Nick and Viola

A Kentucky family tragedy in
the Tobacco Wars (1904-1911)

⟨⟨⟨⟩⟩⟩

By Laura Muntz Derr

Barbara - Hope this story
holds as much meaning
for you as it did for me,

    Laura M. Derr

"Blessed are the poor in spirit,
for theirs is the kingdom of heaven."

Matthew 5:3

To my mother,
who understood family matters

Table of Contents

List of Photographs and Illustrations vii

Acknowledgments xi

Introduction xiii

One: Ancestors 1

Two: Spring Planting 9

Three: Stand Pat 17

Four: Show Your Colors 33

Five: Glorious News 39

Six: Women's World 51

Seven: Night Riders 63

Eight: Burned Out 73

Nine: Shot Down 81

Ten: Consequences 91

Eleven: Unraveling 103

Twelve: Descendants 111

Reflections 143

Notes 155

Bibliography 171

List of Photographs and Illustrations

Joseph Muntz Family Tree xvii

Joseph Muntz, Jr. Family Photo 4
Circa 1896. Muntz homestead in Harrison County, Kentucky, on Salem Pike. Front row, left to right: Joseph Muntz Jr.; Elbert Muntz, son of second marriage; Elizabeth Benson Muntz, second wife of Joseph. Photo inserted in front: Linnia Muntz, daughter of second marriage.

Back row, standing, left to right: Jacob Muntz, brother of Joseph; James Louie Muntz, Roy Harland Muntz, Walter Frank Muntz, George Nicholas Muntz, Joseph Aaron Muntz, all sons of Joseph's first marriage to Armilda White Muntz; Mollie Kate Whitaker Muntz and baby Joseph Muntz, wife and son of Joseph Aaron Muntz; Laura E. Muntz, daughter of Joseph's first marriage to Armilla White.

Viola Judy Muntz and Unidentified Child Photo 6
Circa 1899

Harrison County, Kentucky Map 16

Roy Muntz Family Photo 115
Circa 1920. Seated in front, left to right: Clay Doan, son of William Henry Doan and nephew of Ruth Muntz; Roy Harland Muntz; Ruth Ellen Doan Muntz; Charles Muntz, son of Nick and Viola Muntz. Standing in back, left to right: Doan Muntz, son of Roy and Ruth Muntz; James Kenneth Muntz, son of Nick and Viola Muntz.

Portrait of Alice Muntz Wilson 120
Circa 1920. Daughter of Nick and Viola Muntz.

Alice Muntz Wilson and Walker Wilson Husband and Wife Photo 121
Circa late 1960s. Left to right: Walker Woods Wilson, Alice Muntz Wilson.

Ray Edward Muntz and Children Photo 126
Circa 1932. Front row: Charles Edward Muntz, son of Ray Edward Muntz and Alleene Wilson Muntz; Ray Edward Muntz, son of Nick and Viola Muntz; Ray Edward Muntz Jr., son of Ray Edward Muntz and Alleene Wilson Muntz. Back: Willie Wilson, son of Alleene Wilson Muntz and William Wilson.

Muntz Family Setting Tobacco Photo . . . 130
Circa 1966. Harrison County, Kentucky, on Connersville Pike. Left to right: Charles Edward Muntz, son of Ray Edward and Alleene Muntz; Ray Edward Muntz, son of Nick and Viola Muntz;

Danny Tod Muntz, son of Charles Edward Muntz and Hedy Shaw Muntz.

Volney Whitaker Family Photo 136
Circa 1925. Shelbyville, Indiana. Back row, left to right: Volney Whitaker, husband of Laura Muntz Whitaker; Laura Muntz Whitaker, wife of Volney Whitaker and sister of Nick Muntz; Clara Muntz, daughter of Nick and Viola Muntz; unidentified man; Frances Brunner, daughter of Volney and Laura Muntz Whitaker; Albert Brunner, husband of Frances Brunner. Front row: Donald Brunner, son of Albert and Frances Brunner.

Acknowledgments

I would not have completed this book without the constant encouragement of my brother, Charlie Muntz. Whenever I saw an obstacle, he provided a solution. He searched bookstores and found out-of-print books, traveled to conduct interviews, and wandered around graveyards and old homesteads with me.

I owe a great debt to Connie Webber, chief deputy with the Harrison County Circuit Clerk's office, who connected me with deeds, wills, marriage certificates, and court proceedings. She even traveled to Frankfort on my behalf to retrieve copies of the proceedings of Nick Muntz's examining trial.

Charline and Warren Wilson provided hospitality and local knowledge about Judy Ridge Road and the property owned by Nick and Viola. They took Charlie and me on tours of Nick and Viola's property, the Judy and Muntz family cemeteries, and the Muntz family homestead. They graciously connected me with the family of Alice Wilson in California.

I greatly benefited from the graduate editing class of Dr. Margaret Morgan, University of North Carolina at Charlotte. Her students reviewed my manuscript as a project and provided me with excellent suggestions both in format and organization. I owe special thanks to Joanna Burgess for her Family Tree design concept.

My college roommate Margaret Verble cajoled me into attending two summer writing workshops at Wesleyan University and Kenyon College, where I submitted my writing to peer review. These experiences gave me the confidence to keep writing.

Numerous readers patiently evaluated the book in different stages. I am grateful for those loving friends. I am especially grateful to Sally Kinney, my high school English teacher, who gave the final manuscript a thorough grammatical review.

Ultimately, without the love and support of my husband, Tom, I would not have had the confidence to keep the vision of this book alive over the eight years since my mother's death.

Introduction

When I was a little girl growing up in Kentucky in the 1950s, burley tobacco was king. It was as much a part of the environment as the air and the trees. Tobacco was not something you considered at a conscious level; it was an absolute, a given. It marked the calendar of our days. In the spring, the skies were filled with smoke from the burning of tobacco beds; in the summer, the broad burley leaf covered acres of ground all around us; in the fall, families labored in the stripping rooms and anxiously watched the prices at tobacco auctions. In homes and businesses, at restaurants and sports events, the air was thick with the fragrance of tobacco.

When we opened a magazine or switched on our Zenith TV, tobacco was there: "LSMFT—Lucky Strike Means Fine Tobacco;" "I'd Walk a Mile for a Camel;" "More Doctors Smoke Camels Than Any Other Cigarette;" "John Wayne, A Camel Fan Goin' on Twenty-Four Years;" The "Marlboro Man;" "Call for Philip Morris;" "For Those with Keen Young Tastes;" "ABC—Always Buy Chesterfield;" "Winston Tastes Good Like a Cigarette Should;" "Viceroys—The Taste That's Right."

All the glamorous people smoked. Ronald Reagan appeared in ads. Doctors recommended certain brands. Smoking created the ritual of romance: the offer of a cigarette, lighting a cigarette, the full inhalation deep into the lungs and out, the spiraling smoke over the heads of a couple deep in conversation. Smoking was patriotic: what soldier, sailor, marine, or pilot in WWII could resist cigarette smoking? Cartons of cigarettes were distributed free to the men and women in uniform. "Smoke 'em if you got 'em" was the mantra of war movies. For baby boomers like me, cigarette smoke is the sensory trigger: Whenever it is breathed in, it says, "Mother, the smell of my mother; Father, the smell of my father." Like an old family album, it conjures up memories of scenes and events.

Unless you have labored in the field to plant the tender shoots, weeded the rows, suckered the tops, squeezed the tobacco worm until it burst, severed the stalks and skewered them onto long tobacco sticks, hung the sticks in the barn on three levels (shingled so the air can pass through), stood in the barn space heavy with a crop of leathery burley; unless you have smelled the pungent leaf, felt its texture, marveled at the variety of leaf along the tobacco stalk; unless you have depended on the success of that crop to release you from debt and waited in the auction house with bated breath to hear the price (knowing it means Christmas for your family); unless you have smoked, chewed, or pinched tobacco and used it more and more as a crutch for everything else in your life that you couldn't control—unless you have lived all that, you can hardly imagine the power of the tobacco leaf in the Bluegrass Region for over a century.

Tobacco changed history. Its economic value brought western European countries into conflict over trade routes and markets. It even played a role in the American Revolution. Tidewater planters in eighteenth-century Virginia, who raised tobacco for British and European markets, became addicted to the lifestyle of the rich. They also became indebted to their agents across the water, building up more and more debt over the years. By 1776 economic distress dovetailed with distress over colonists' rights.[1] Later, tobacco was a factor in the Civil War. Tobacco reinforced the logic of slavery, since the rigors of raising and housing tobacco on large plantations required cheap manpower.

Tobacco made some men rich and reduced others to poverty. Today Duke University is an elite educational institution. The money that endowed it flowed from the fortune of James Duke, who in the early 1900s monopolized the manufacture of tobacco, set prices below the cost of production, and triggered the populist tobacco wars in Tennessee and Kentucky.[2]

Tobacco changed my family history. This book is the story of Viola and Nick Muntz, who lived in Harrison County, Kentucky, in the early 1900s. It is the story of the tobacco wars that affected the lives of all tobacco growers during that time.

It is also my story. I grew up in the 1950s and 1960s in a world still dominated by tobacco culture. When my mother began researching genealogy in the 1980s, she unlocked the mystery of the Muntz family. The stories that she unearthed are much more important to me today than they once were. Now it is my turn to remember and value the lives of those who otherwise may be forgotten.

Joseph Muntz, Sr. Family Tree 1809-2012

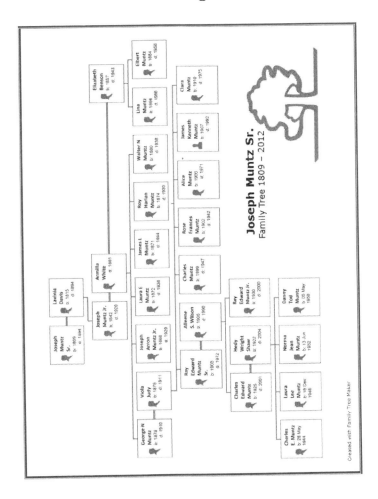

Joseph Muntz Sr.
Family Tree 1809 – 2012

Created with Family Tree Maker

.

CHAPTER ONE

Ancestors

Tombstones rarely tell the truth. They present a respectable face, cite name and dates and sometimes a pious homily, but they leave the hard truths about lives unsaid.

In rural Harrison County, Kentucky, just off the Republican Pike, a small, well-tended cemetery surrounds a country church. Located in the tiny community of Buena Vista, Republican Christian Church sits on the top of a hill looking out over rolling pastureland. The current structure, built in 1924, is red brick, but two other log structures preceded it. Walking around, I am struck by the ages of the stones, some of them nearly two hundred years old. Among the stones, two sit side by side, just to the west of the church. White and worn, they bear these fading inscriptions:

Viola Muntz	George N. Muntz
Born March 22, 1875	Born Feb. 20, 1878
Died Apr. 23, 1911	Died Feb. 11, 1910

Neither grave bears an epitaph. On this summer weekday visit in 2006, the cemetery is a peaceful place. The only sounds are birds calling back and forth and the occasional car going by. The view to the north draws my eyes to the distant horizon and the faraway rolling hills. This space feels separate and apart from the world. Perhaps it has been a good place for Nick and Viola to settle after their short, turbulent lives together.

My great-grandfather, George Nicholas "Nick" Muntz, was a tobacco farmer. He lived all his thirty-two years in Harrison County, Kentucky, in the Bluegrass Region of the state. Nick grew up in the eastern part of the county, near Oddville. In 1898, when he married Viola Judy, he moved farther east on Judy Ridge Road. According to the federal census of 1910, Nick and Viola were landowners and farmed about forty-seven acres. They had six children over a period of eleven years. Like many others around them, they raised burley tobacco. These details would ordinarily be of interest mainly to genealogists and family historians, except for the fact that neither Nick nor Viola lived to see their children grow up. In the early 1900s, their lives were caught up in the violence in Kentucky known as the tobacco wars.

Nick and Viola's story could not have been predicted from their family backgrounds. By the time

Nick was born, the Muntz family was two genera-
tions old in the United States. Its men were soldiers
and survivors. According to a history of Harrison
County, Nick's great-grandfather Jacob, a native of
Prussia, served in the Austrian Lancers and fought
against Napoleon. Nick's grandfather Joseph Muntz
Sr. was born in 1809 and emigrated from Baden,
Germany, to America through the Port of New
Orleans in 1836.[3]

Nick's father, Joseph Muntz Jr., was born in 1842.
He was a Union soldier in the Civil War and served
in Company D. 7th, Kentucky Cavalry, from 1862 to
1865. Joseph was captured by John Hunt Morgan
at the first Battle of Cynthiana, just six days after he
enlisted in July, before he had even been sworn in.
He was sent to Camp Chase, Ohio, but he somehow
managed to return home eighteen days later, having
walked the whole way. Later he fought in engage-
ments in east Tennessee and was injured, though not
in battle. While camping in Chattanooga, Georgia,
Joseph's feet, wrapped in a gum blanket, were badly
burned as he slept in front of a fire.[4]

This incident did not end his military career.
After ten days in the hospital, he joined his company
again and was involved in many skirmishes until
the close of the war and "endured several forced
marches…one of which…covered three hundred
miles in six days."[5] At the end of the war, Joseph was
among a party of men "detailed to capture Jeffer-
son Davis," but history gives credit for the capture to
the Fourth Michigan Company under the command

of Colonel Pritchard. Mustered out in 1865, Joseph came home and married Armilla White in 1867. As is typical, there is no history of women in Harrison County, so little is known about her except that she had two children at the time of their marriage and became the mother of six more children by Joseph, including Nick, before she died in 1881. Joseph then married Elizabeth Benson, and they had two more children.

In a family picture, probably taken between 1896 and 1898, Joseph and his family sit in front of their farmhouse.[6] Of the thirteen people in the picture, Joseph and Elizabeth are the only two seated, surrounded by the members of their blended families. Even seated, Joseph is a formidable man, tall and muscular with a full head of black hair and a mustache. He appears to be a prosperous landowner and family man. Behind him to his right stands Nick, about eighteen years old, a stocky young man ready to take up the reins of his own life.

JOSEPH MUNTZ, JR. FAMILY

Viola Judy's family had a longer history as Americans than Nick's. Descended from Martin Tschude, who emigrated from Switzerland in 1767, her ancestors had been living in the United States for four generations by the time of her birth in 1875. It was Martin's son David (Viola's grandfather) who anglicized the family name to Judy. Viola's father, James Judy, appears to have been well established as a property owner. Deed transfer records show his heirs receiving large tracts of land around Beaver Creek.[7] Viola was the second youngest of five children, the only daughter, with four brothers: Charles, Virgil, James, and George.

Only one picture of Viola has survived, and it has been cut out of a larger photograph. In this fragment, a lovely young woman sits with her arm around a standing child, perhaps three or four years old. Even though the child wears a long dress, the haircut suggests a boy. Family tradition states that this child is my grandfather Ray. If that is true, Viola would be thirty-four years old in this picture, yet she looks much younger. The younger child is more likely Charlie, her firstborn when she was twenty-four. Still this image seems far too youthful, and it may be Viola posing with another young family member. Her dress, posture, and demeanor suggest a favored child, the only daughter in a prosperous family who grew up to be an attractive young woman, expecting that life would continue to favor her.

VIOLA JUDY MUNTZ AND UNIDENTIFIED CHILD

Where did Viola and Nick meet? Did they first glance at one another at a church social at Republican Christian Church? Did they grow up going to school together? Since she was three years older than Nick, when would they have first looked at each other as peers? However they managed to meet, they must have fallen in love and found a way to be together, for she and Nick married on October 13, 1898. Their first child, Charlie, was born on March 22, 1899.

Viola owned the land where she and Nick lived after their marriage. She held title to 44.34 acres of land along Beaver Creek facing Judy Ridge Road. Harrison County Court records show that Viola sold this land to her brother James on March 1, 1899, "in consideration of one dollar."[8] On the same day, James sold 47.34 acres to Viola for one dollar. Local lore explains this land swap as a friendly family deal. Viola inherited land from her father that bordered on Judy Ridge Road, but she did not want to live directly on the road. So she swapped parcels with James. Viola was a smart trader. She not only received more land in the swap, she also received the family home and a barn. In 1899 Viola and Nick's future looked bright compared to many young couples setting up households.

Like most of their generation in rural Kentucky, Nick and Viola were farmers, specifically tobacco farmers. Although they probably raised several crops to feed themselves and their animals, the main money crop was tobacco. At the turn of the century, no other crop could realize an income of eight to twelve dollars per hundred pounds[9]. Even though raising tobacco required backbreaking work, it returned a reliable and predictable income. Nick and Viola probably raised about five acres of tobacco, the most they could cultivate on their own. Five acres would bring in around four hundred dollars in family income.[10] Tenant farmers had to split that income with the landlord, but landowners could keep the whole check, or at least what was left of it after paying off the bills. So Nick and Viola, living alongside Beaver Creek, had the prospect of a good life together.

But that prospect did not take into account James Duke, owner of the American Tobacco Company, who created a monopoly that, by 1905, cut prices paid for tobacco down to six to seven dollars per hundred pounds.[11] Economic desperation followed and set into motion a tragic chain of events for Nick and Viola and their family.

Over the years the story of Nick and Viola was lost. Eventually my mother became interested in genealogy and began to research the history of the Muntz family. She uncovered the story of Pa Muntz's parents, Nick and Viola, and their tragic involvement in the tobacco wars. She gave my dad the story of his ancestors, lost through shame and the disintegration of Viola and Nick's family. This story is not an easy family album to leaf through, but it is the testimony of those who came before us, whose suffering and sacrifice forged the identities we have today.

CHAPTER TWO

Spring Planting

In the early 1900s, Nick and Viola's family grew. Alice was born on April 2, 1900, and Rose followed on September 10, 1902. Baby Ray arrived on April 12, 1905. With an expanding family, Nick and Viola depended on their burley tobacco cash crop. During those years the prices for burley fluctuated but still provided a reliable source of income to growers.

In order to raise five acres of tobacco, the maximum amount an independent grower could manage without tenant farmers, Nick and Viola needed the hands of family and neighbors at the two crucial times of the season—spring planting and fall harvesting. Numerous Muntz relatives throughout Harrison County probably helped. Viola's brothers, Ed,

Virgil, and James, lived nearby or on adjacent property; neighbors David and Minnie Coy lived across the road. David Coy suffered from tuberculosis and could no longer handle the hard physical labor of farm work, but the Coys had five children, four of whom were boys. Robert, Elva, and John Bill, the three older boys, likely partnered with Nick and Viola, borrowing their team of horses and sharing the tasks of raising tobacco. Along Judy Ridge Road were other neighbors: Milt Florence, Hub Wyles, and Boss Garrison. The communal requirements of raising tobacco no doubt made these farmers allies during busy seasons.

The first task of spring—planting the seedbeds—actually began in the late fall or winter. Nick had to stake out and plow the area he needed for the beds before the ground froze. He had to choose a good site for his tobacco seedbeds, probably somewhere along Beaver Creek which meandered through his farm. According to written accounts from early in the century, the best site for a tobacco bed was one that sloped gently, bordered a water source, and enjoyed a southern exposure.[12] After plowing the ground, Nick had to pile brush and logs on the site, making sure they were high enough to stay dry until he was ready to burn them. Sometime between late February and March 15 (depending on the signs of spring and the *Farmer's Almanac*), Nick burned his tobacco beds, tending the fire all day and into the evening until only embers were left. Burning the beds killed any pests or diseases in the soil and created a nourishing home for the tiny tobacco seeds. While waiting for the fires to burn down, he was probably visited by neighbors. In the cold early spring, burning fires and smoke rising up in the sky made a cheerful sight and smell, beckoning people to stop by and share their hopes for the growing season.

When the fuel had burned down to ash the next day, Nick pulled off any logs that had not completely burned and smoothed the ashes over the soil of the bed. With the ashes, which provided nutrition, he probably mixed in manure to help the seeds germinate and grow. Undoubtedly he created more than one seedbed to provide plants maturing at different times. Even with neighbors working together, planting could take weeks, depending on weather conditions. A good supply of mature, vigorous plants was essential to setting the crop out.

The tobacco seeds Nick planted were so small that 300 to 400,000 were contained in an ounce. When sown, one ounce of seed yielded as many as 40,000 plants, and a seedbed of 500 square yards was required to yield about 10,000 plants.[13] According to the 1911 *Encyclopaedia Britannica,* "an acre of tobacco…will contain…10,000 plants."[14] If Nick was planting five acres, he would have needed about 50,000 plants. Thus he could carry all the seed he would need for the year's crop in a bag in his pocket.

After clearing and smoothing the burnt ground, Nick took his bag of tiny seed and mixed it with some of the ashes in order to sow it more evenly. Following the tradition of the day, he cast half of this mixture across the bed while walking in one direction and recast the other half over the same soil while walking in the other direction. Finally he covered the bed with muslin and staked it down on the sides to shelter the tender plants as they emerged from the soil. Having done everything he could to prepare his beds, he waited.

It must have lifted Nick's spirits to approach the tobacco beds early in May and see the vigorous young plants pushing up against the white muslin, ready to be pulled and set. Turning back the cover, he could see the whole year's bounty awaiting his hands. The sun shone brightly and the season of growing beckoned him. Surely he felt a moment of peace and connection, a kingdom of heaven moment, when the whole world seemed to have conspired to bring everything into perfect conjunction and harmony. But the moment was brief, for the tiny plants had to be separated and set into rows to become massive fields of burley.

Pulling plants was the next step in setting the tobacco, after preparing the soil with horse and plow. The rule was never to pull more plants than could be set in a day, for once a plant wilted, its survival was compromised. Nick probably filled water buckets from Beaver Creek to hold the plants' tender roots. It was important to dig gently around under the roots of the plants, pull out a block of plants at one time, and separate them into individual sets. With an ample supply of plants for the day, he was ready to set tobacco.

Tobacco plants could not be set out until after the last frost, and to be safe that was around May 15. By that time spring planting was in full swing, and there was not enough daylight between sunup and sundown to accomplish all that growers needed to do. The window of time for planting was fairly narrow, about a month to six weeks between mid-May and the end of June. If the crop was planted too early, there was still danger of frostbite. If it was planted too late, it was more vulnerable to tobacco worms in August and could not be harvested until far into the fall.

Of course, no matter when the crop was set out, the rains had to cooperate for it to thrive. The weather was surely a topic of everyday conversation between Nick and Viola, as it was for every farm family. Viola likely kept a daily diary of the weather, worrying when the crop needed rain and rejoicing when it came.

In 1900 Nick and his neighbors may have had to hand-set their crops. Hand-setting required two people: one who walked through the row using a tool that created a depression in the ground and another who dropped the plants in one at a time. Nick may have had access to a mechanical setter since he and Viola owned a team of horses. In those days a good team of horses was a source of pride. Farmers bragged about the ability of their teams to set a straight row and avoid stepping on tender new plants.

The mechanical setter was an ingenious device. Pulled by the horse, it created a hole, dropped the plants at measured intervals, and squirted a drink of water into each depression. For mechanical tobacco setting, three people were required: one on the front of the setter to steer the horse, one to drop the plants into the rotating setting wheel on the back, and one to follow and tightly tap down the newly set plant into its bed with a hoe or foot. It was slow, tedious work that numbed the shoulders and the back, but it was still far superior to old-fashioned hand-setting.

Nick might have had the use of a lister cultivator as well. The lister was a double-moldboard plow that allowed a farmer to create hills and trenches along the rows where the plants would be set. Planting on hills allowed the tobacco plants to drain well, even after hard rains.

Whatever the tools at hand, Nick and his neighbors worked out in the fields for days and weeks, starting at dawn and dragging home at dusk—dirty, hungry, and exhausted.

Viola was left at home alone with the babies and the household tasks. In 1902 she had no running water or electricity, for water lines had not yet come out from town, and the Rural Electrification Administration would not become a reality until Franklin Delano Roosevelt's New Deal in the 1930s. To cook, Viola had to start a fire in the woodstove in the kitchen; moreover, she needed an almost mystical understanding of temperature and timing for baking. To wash clothes, she had to boil enough water to fill a washtub. Using lye soap and a washboard, she had to hand-scrub every garment, rinse them in another tub, and run them through a hand wringer. The only dryer she had was a clothesline, and in the cold months of winter and early spring, every garment she hung out would freeze and ultimately had to be thawed inside.

In addition to such routine chores, Viola would have had chickens to feed and eggs to gather, and probably a cow to milk. Without refrigeration, the milk required a whole group of chores in itself. It had to be left to set until the cream could be skimmed off and churned into butter. The leftover buttermilk was a favorite drink with a meal of soup beans and cornbread. Of course Viola was also responsible for the meals, and by early spring she would have used up the last of the winter's canning and root vegetables. Factored into all these chores was the daily care of the children and the isolation of farm life. While the men labored in community, women worked alone.

Hopefully Nick and Viola had a social and religious life. Perhaps families and neighbors gathered occasionally to share their news and stories. Perhaps Nick and Viola attended church regularly and found comfort in the pews of Republican Christian Church. But from day to day, like most of their contemporaries, their lives were ordered by the demands of the tobacco crop, and it was a hard taskmaster.

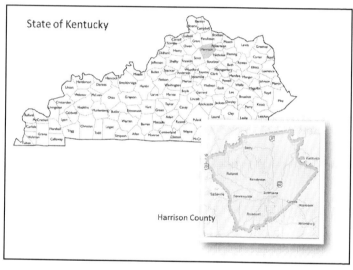

HARRISON COUNTY, KENTUCKY MAP

CHAPTER THREE

Stand Pat

By 1906 the downward spiral of tobacco prices had become intolerable. No matter how hard they worked, tobacco farmers saw the value of their crops diminish. Nick and Viola were among the many whose livelihoods depended on a marketplace controlled by one company in North Carolina, the American Tobacco Company (ATC), also known as the "Trust."[15] The ATC was owned by one man, James Buchanan Duke. Today the Duke name is associated with philanthropy and a fine university, but in the early 1900s James Duke was a brilliant and ruthless businessman, determined to monopolize the tobacco market in the United States.

Born in 1856 on a farm near Durham, North Carolina, James Duke grew up in a Methodist family. His father, Washington Duke, started a tobacco company after the Civil War, and James took over the business in the 1880s. Duke realized that the profits from selling plug chewing tobacco were stagnant, and he believed the future of the tobacco industry was in cigarettes.[16] The problem with cigarettes was production; at that time they were hand-rolled, so labor costs were high. In 1880, when James Bonsack invented a machine that could mass-produce cigarettes, Duke entered into an agreement with the Bonsack Company to use only Bonsack machines in his manufacturing. He negotiated a reduced royalty fee for his company and an agreement that Bonsack would sell machines only to the top five tobacco companies: W. Duke and Sons, Kinney Tobacco Company, Allen and Ginter, William S. Kimball, and Goodwin and Company.[17] This agreement prohibited start-up companies from taking advantage of the Bonsack technology.

Then James Duke started a price war against the other four major companies. "In such wars, a given product was named a 'battle brand,' the price of which was cut below its cost."[18] In order to compete, the other companies had to reduce their prices drastically, often selling their products for less than they cost to produce. Since Duke had more profits from other brands, he could outlast the other companies. As their deficits mounted, Duke offered to purchase the companies on generous terms. "In October 1889 an agreement was settled merging the five companies into one, The American Tobacco Company."[19]

Next the American Tobacco Company set its sights on local companies throughout tobacco-producing regions. Over the next few years, it bought out or drove out of business more than 250 separate tobacco manufacturers.[20] While keeping the local names, the ATC set the price these companies paid for growers' tobacco crops. By 1906 the ATC held an absolute monopoly over price, which would not be legally challenged until 1911, when the company was found to be in violation of the Sherman Antitrust Act.[21]

By the time of James Duke's death in 1925, he was a fabulously wealthy man. He established the Duke Endowment, donating $107 million to programs that benefited children, health care, higher education, and rural churches in North Carolina. The website for the Duke Endowment features the phrase "Spirit of Genius, Legacy of Hope." Duke University was one of the first institutions of higher education to include women as students. Ironically, great good has come out of the Duke fortune, but great hardship and even tragedy resulted for tobacco growers in the early 1900s, as James Duke methodically squeezed every penny of profit out of tobacco production in Kentucky and Tennessee.

In December 1906 the range of tobacco prices reported in *The Log Cabin* newspaper was four dollars per hundred pounds to seventeen dollars per hundred pounds, but the lower end of the range was far more likely.[22] Farmers, who lived indebted most of the year and paid off their debts when they sold their crops, could not break even, let alone make a profit. Understandably, many began to agitate for change.

Unrest first occurred in the Black Patch area of western and south central Kentucky and northern Tennessee. [23] The Planters Protective Association (PPA), formed in the Black Patch area, was already making headlines in 1904. The PPA organized and attempted to pool tobacco crops and hold them off the market to be sold as one unit for a higher price. The larger and more prosperous growers devised the plan, but it required a high percentage of unity on the part of all growers to succeed. James Duke cleverly manipulated smaller independent farmers by offering to privately purchase their crops for high sums, sight unseen. As a result the ability of the PPA to negotiate with the American Tobacco Company on behalf of all growers was compromised. Desperate growers, after holding their tobacco off the market for at least two years, turned to violence. Although never sanctioned by the official PPA, bands of masked men known as "night riders" destroyed tobacco beds, threatened and even beat and killed growers to convince them to pool their tobacco. They burned enormous warehouses of tobacco purchased by the ATC and terrorized the regions where they operated.[24] Until 1906 the central and northern regions of Kentucky, where white burley was grown, did not experience this populist uprising. But their economic situation was parallel, and they too began to organize.

Throughout the growing season in 1906, *The Log Cabin* carried reports of an early attempt at organizing, the Kentucky and Ohio Burley Tobacco Growers Company.[25] This organization failed to unite burley growers around the idea of cutting crop production to force higher prices, and in July the paper carried reports of plans to dissolve the company and pay back stockholders any unspent funds. But by October the newspaper reported a meeting planned for November in Winchester to reorganize the growers.

This time the burley growers united with a national organization named the American Society of Equity (ASE), a group dedicated to various populist causes, including the right of the tobacco farmer to a fair price for his crop. As the result of a meeting on November 3, 1906, local delegates from several Bluegrass counties came home determined to canvass their neighbors for pledges to pool the 1906 tobacco crop and sell it as one entity to the American Tobacco Company. Their action led to impassioned speeches at several meetings and to letters carried in *The Log Cabin*. The controversy stirred up local emotional resolve to fight James Duke and the ATC monopoly. One letter, under the headline "Stand Pat," was printed on November 23, just before the first Burley Tobacco Society organizational meeting in Harrison County:

...December 1st, will find us twenty thousand strong, and this time with an army that has burned its bridges after crossing over. We are profiting by the mistakes made heretofore. We do not need any money to buy this tobacco, for we already own it....

Speaking of burning our bridges behind us, what does that mean?

It means that we growers say to Mr. Duke, you have not treated us right since you have been setting the price for us. We have not received a fair living price for our tobacco, and so we have organized (we the damn fool farmers you call us), have organized for 15 cents tobacco. You will either pay 15 cents for good Burley tobacco or get no tobacco....

This will be a fight to the finish....

The larger the pool the stronger.

The larger the pool the sooner we will sell....

Let no one lag behind.

Let's be up and doing.

Someone has been setting a price on your tobacco for years. It isn't just.

Someone says you won't stick.

I say the tobacco grower is the greatest sticker on earth.

He sticks out a plant in the spring and works and sticks to that plant fourteen hours a day, until he

puts it on a stick in the fall. Then
he is continually handling it off
and on the stick, until he sticks it
on the market, and then frequently
gets stuck: and in the end when he
counts up his time, he has worked
fourteen hours a day, and fourteen
months in a year, and has nothing to
show for it, except that he has stuck
to it like a man.

Now if the grower will stick to an
infernal tobacco plant like that, I
know he will stick to the organization when it guarantees him 15 cents
per pound for a good merchantable
crop of tobacco.

I am from Missouri and you will
have to show me that he won't.

Yours truly,
HENRY E. SWAN, Sec'y.,
Burley Tobacco Society

In early December 1906, county representatives met at Winchester. Clarence LeBus, one of
the wealthiest tobacco growers in central Kentucky,
attended as chairman from Harrison County. The
new organization was named the Burley Tobacco
Society (BTS), a "branch of the American Society
of Equity, Department of Tobacco Growers."[26] At
that meeting officers were elected and a new pledge
was adopted. Farmers would be asked to sign this
pledge to pool their tobacco. It committed them to
pool their crops with the BTS, allowing the Society
to grade, handle, and sell the tobacco on their behalf

for no less than fifteen cents a pound. Farmers who signed were only bound to this pledge if 50 percent or more of the crop grown was pledged to the pool by January 1907.[27]

The Harrison County meeting took place on Saturday, December 8, 1906, at the courthouse in Cynthiana. According to *The Log Cabin*, "A large crowd of farmers filled the court house to overflowing…and a large number were unable to secure seats."[28] Clarence LeBus spoke to the crowd on behalf of the reorganized Burley Tobacco Society. LeBus was short in stature, had piercing gray eyes; a strong, jutting chin; and, according to the *Lexington Leader* newspaper, "a backbone as big as a telephone pole."[29] A wealthy landlord, LeBus had tenants or sharecroppers who raised tobacco on his land and received half the proceeds from the crop for their labor. Though he could not commit his tenants at that time, LeBus announced that he had signed over all his tobacco over to the Society (about 1,200,000 pounds) and urged those present to do the same. "Mr. LeBus declared that it was the farmers' own fault if they failed to get 15 cents for their tobacco this year."[30]

At this meeting a precinct committee was formed and appointed committeemen to canvass growers in the rural communities of Oddville, Elmarch, Sylvan Dell,[31] Leesburg, Park, Lair, Belmont, Tricum, Kinman, Colemansville, Berry, Richland, Claysville, and Poindexter. Canvassers were urged not only to bring back signatures of growers who signed the pledge, but also to keep a list of those who did not, supposedly to make sure the pool could prove 50 percent or more committed in the county.[32] A list of those who did not sign the pledge could also be a useful tool to isolate and pressure those farmers to change their minds.

As these events were taking place, *The Log Cabin* reported various tobacco sales. In Lexington, according to the December 7 newspaper, "100,000 pounds of tobacco sold at the loose tobacco warehouses... Tuesday at an average of 10 cents per pound. $13.50 [per hundred pounds] was the highest price paid."[33] On December 14 the newspaper reported that "Tobacco of a high grade continues to sell at a high price, some of the material offered at Tuesday morning's sale going as high as 17c [*sic*] a pound.... Among the heavy bidders the American Tobacco Company is...buying all grades and as much of each as is possible."[34] Even as farmers were uniting to force a fair price for their crops, the American Tobacco Company was undermining their individual wills by offering unusually high prices for crops brought to the auction warehouses. The battle was joined, and so began the tobacco war in the burley area of Kentucky, one that would peak in 1908 and would not completely subside until the Burley Tobacco Society disbanded in 1911.

Nick and Viola lived in the Sylvan Dell precinct of Harrison County. The canvassers for that area in December 1906 were neighbors Herbert Wyles, D.E. McCauley, and J.M. Florence. One of them probably came calling, in the waning days of December, to urge Nick to sign the tobacco pledge and pool his crop. They probably also stopped next door at the farm of Viola's brother, Ed Judy, and across the road at Minnie Coy's place. Or perhaps they invited all their neighbors to come and hear Clarence LeBus give one of several speeches he made in Sunrise, Leesburg, and Cynthiana.

It is hard to know how much Nick and Viola Muntz and their neighbors, with the argument swirling all around them, debated this growing furor for change. Certainly the newspapers were full of the story, and telephones were in use at that time, though few rural homes had one. Although radios had not yet appeared in rural households, everyone must have been talking about Clarence LeBus and the pros and cons of pooling.

During November and December, most farmers were in their stripping rooms preparing their crops for auction. The work of stripping tobacco was exhaustive and all consuming, but it was also social. Often neighbors and family members banded together to help each other strip the leaves off tobacco stalks and prepare them for market. They spent months together standing along the stripping room table, sorting and tying hands of tobacco. There was plenty of time to talk about local gossip, stories in the newspaper, and opinions of those who had attended the courthouse meeting on December 8. Most likely they had long and passionate conversations about the tobacco pledge and the Burley Tobacco Society.

This stripping process was the final tedious step in the laborious production of a tobacco crop. Before the work of stripping, the exhausting work of cutting and housing tobacco from the field had to take place. In September Nick and his neighbors watched the weather to make sure they had enough days without rain to hand-cut the massive burley stalks, spear the stalks onto tobacco sticks, and lay the sticks onto wagons in the field. The loaded wagons were then pulled by horses to the barn, where three sets of tobacco rails divided the barn into levels. A man worked off the wagon and handed the tobacco sticks to a man on the first rail, the hottest place in the barn. The man on the first rail handed it up to the man on the second rail, who did the same to the man on the third rail. The third and highest rail was the most dangerous position for a laborer in the harvesting process. When the tobacco sticks filled the tiers of the third rail, the top man stepped down and helped fill the second rail, and then finally the first, until the barn was full. Care had to be taken to shingle the tobacco sticks so that none of the tobacco on the higher rail hung directly on top of the tobacco below, blocking the air that flowed among the stalks. The end result was a barn hung full of fragrant burley stalks, six or more stalks to a tobacco stick laid across the barn rafters two stories high.

By the end of a day housing tobacco, men felt an exhaustion that started in their necks and worked all the way down to their toes. Arms became like stumps, burning and sore. Backs were stretched to the point of breaking. Nick and his family and neighbors repeated this process until all their crops were housed, probably devoting the month of September to getting all the tobacco into the barn.

Then over the next two months they harvested their corn and waited for tobacco to come "in case." Art and experience were involved in knowing the right moment tobacco was in case.[35] The leaves had to absorb enough moisture so they could be handled without crumbling, but they also could not be so moist that they would rot when piled on the barn floor for stripping. Outside the Bluegrass, farmers used coke-burning stoves to cure the tobacco hanging in their barns, reducing the moisture content until the tobacco was "in case" with just the right leathery texture. But in central Kentucky, farmers used nature's method, constructing two-story barns with long vertical side-vent doors that could be opened to the air and breezes to cure the excess moisture out of their crop.

Undoubtedly Nick visited his barn regularly after housing his tobacco to breathe in the aromatic bounty of eight months' making. The long cool rains that brought the last leaves off the trees and turned the fallen walnuts black on the ground also created the right moisture conditions to handle the massive hanging stalks of burley. Finally the burley would be ready to be handed down, pulled off the sticks, stripped from the stalks, graded, and tied into hands.

In those days stripping tobacco was an art form, very different from the current process in which tobacco is packed into bales and sold by weight. In fact, the process has come full circle, for in the 1800s most tobacco was packed and sold in hogsheads, large thousand-pound barrels into which tobacco was compressed, or "prized," so it could be shipped to market and stored for up to two years for manufacture.[36] From colonial times until the early twentieth century, farmers had to transport their tobacco to markets far away, even overseas. Probably Nick's father, Joseph, had to send his tobacco to market prized into hogsheads that were rolled and pulled by horses. By the time Nick was growing tobacco, roads had improved, railroad connections were extensive, and warehouses for tobacco auctions were located locally.

By the early 1900s, a new "loose-leaf" process of preparation had begun to be preferred, both by buyers and tobacco growers whose crops were of high quality. This method of stripping came about in conjunction with easier access to markets. With the loose-leaf method, farmers stripped the stalks, sorted leaves by grade, tied "hands" of leaves together, and then laid them on round baskets for viewing. Buyers could see what they were buying, and the grower would fetch a better price for his quality crop. According to reports in *The Log Cabin*, both methods were still in use in the early 1900s.[37]

Sorting tobacco into grades required experience and skill. Some farmers sorted into as many as seven or eight groups, but most would use five: trash, lugs, light, dark or red, and tips. All grades had an economic value, though in different seasons some grades were in more demand than others. As one farmer put it, "The fine grades are used for cigarettes. As you get up the stalk and into the reds you get either chewing or pipe tobacco. The leaves on the lower part of the plant are the mildest, and that's what's used for cigarettes."[38] No matter what the grade, all of the leaves were tied and sent to auction. In the stripping room, the most experienced hand stood at the head of the table and stripped the trash (bottom leaves) off the stalk, then passed it down to the next hand, where the lugs were removed, and so on, until the stalk reached the end of the table with nothing left on it except the tips, to be stripped off by the least experienced hand. When a stripper had a handful of leaves in a pile, he or she took another leaf and tied it neatly around the group to form a hand of tobacco, which would then be mounted on a tobacco stick extending horizontally from the stripping room table.

The final step in the stripping process was the tobacco press. A tobacco stick could usually hold twelve to fourteen tied hands. The full tobacco stick was placed in a homemade tobacco press and compressed to flatten the leaves and help keep them "in case" longer.[39] Finally the sticks of tobacco were piled on a wagon and transported to market, where a sample of the farmer's hands was arranged on round baskets to show off the quality leaf to the best advantage.

Although women often helped in tobacco stripping, it would have been hard for Viola to participate while her children were still so young. Even Charlie, the oldest, was only seven in 1906. More likely her job was to provide food for the workers—not the massive meals she prepared for the harvesters when they broke for lunch from the fields, but pails of cold offerings the workers could eat in the barn, taking less time away from their work.

Over those long weeks together, Nick and his coworkers became a community, gossiping, arguing, laughing, and telling stories. Perhaps they agreed that organizing a pool was a lost cause, even though they cursed James B. Duke and hoped against hope for a crop price this year that would pay off the bills and leave a little money for Christmas. With the advantage of history and hindsight, it is tempting today to judge those who chose to continue raising and selling tobacco in spite of the pooling efforts of the BTS. But at the time, children had to be fed and clothed, the pooling outcome was unclear, and skepticism and independence were understandable. The Muntzes and the Judys were immigrants and survivors; they depended on each other more than outsiders. And they did not pool their tobacco.

CHAPTER FOUR

Show Your Colors

In the early days of 1907, thanks to relentless local canvassing, nearly 60 percent of the growers in the forty burley-producing counties of the Bluegrass pledged to pool tobacco with the Burley Tobacco Society. Clarence LeBus was elected president of the society.[40] In Harrison County the County Board of Control, also headed by LeBus, initiated plans for forming the Harrison County Tobacco Company; creating stock; and setting up a system for storing, grading, and selling the poolers' crops.[41] From this point on, Clarence LeBus's name was synonymous with the poolers and the BTS.

In February 1907 pooling advocates harangued independents to join the tobacco pool. The pledge that poolers urged them to sign appeared in *The Log Cabin* on February 1:

We, the undersigned, for, and in consideration for the benefits to be derived from having our tobacco handled and sold by the Burley Tobacco Society, a branch of the American Society of Equity, do hereby pledge to the said Society the number of acres of tobacco set opposite our names, raised during the season of 1907,which constitutes our entire crop, and do constitute it to our agent for the purpose of receiving, grading, handling and selling the same on such terms as the Society may prescribe in accordance with its charter and laws.

PROVIDED: The said Society shall not sell or otherwise dispose of said tobacco for less than the minimum price of fifteen cents per pound for an average crop.[42]

Nick Muntz and his brother-in-law, Ed Judy, did not sign the pledge. The early months of 1907 were uncommonly cold, with reports of temperatures as low as nine below zero. Viola was pregnant with their fifth child, Kenneth, who would be born in August. Their two oldest children, Charlie and Alice, were school-age; Rose was four, and Ray was almost two. The hard realities of daily living would have given anyone pause at the idea of holding the family's main cash crop off the market. Perhaps Nick and Ed did not trust the organizers, even though several of their neighbors joined the pool. Perhaps they embraced the economic opportunity, for the American Tobacco Company was offering high prices to those who refused to pool their crops. For whatever reasons, like other independents in the silent minority, they did not pool their tobacco.

The organizers of the Burley Tobacco Society publicly opposed the violence against independents in the Black Patch area of Kentucky, but at the same time, they made strong remarks about the motives of those who did not join. J. B. Berry, a manager of the Harrison County Tobacco Company, wrote in a letter to *The Log Cabin* in March 1907 that the independents "have grown so selfish that, while they have sold for better prices by our efforts, [they] are not willing that we should get what our goods are worth."[43] In April Berry threatened the independents in a fiery article under the headline "Show Your Colors":

> The time has come for the tobacco growers of the Burley district to show their colors, whether they are with the tillers of the soil…or whether they are against all interests of themselves and neighbors. In order to show how we stand on this matter, we will at the proper time publish in county papers the names of all Harrison County farmers who are with our tobacco movement, and all who are against our, and their, interests.[44]

Emotions were running high, but no violence had occurred yet in the Bluegrass Region. Daily news stories, however, catalogued the violence that was occurring in the Black Patch, where night riders had turned the countryside into a place of vigilante lawlessness, burning barns and enormous stores of tobacco purchased by the ATC, destroying tobacco beds and beating and even killing independents who did not pool their tobacco.

In April 1907 the Harrison County Committee of the Burley Growers Association celebrated the fact that 80 to 90 percent of the crop in Harrison had been pooled, joining other county representatives at a massive barbecue in Lexington.[45] Meanwhile independents like Nick kept their own counsel, quietly burning their tobacco beds and preparing to plant a crop to sell in the fall.

As the year progressed, the tense spring turned into a sweltering summer. Tobacco plants set out in May and June now required cultivation. Nick hoped for a uniform field of green healthy leaves, but he had to deal with numerous threats throughout the growing season. Weeds, blooms, suckers, tobacco worms, and diseases were all part of the cycle of growth. Continual physical effort was required to manage these issues.

To control weeds and keep the ground mounded around the stalks and loose enough so it could drink in moisture, the tobacco had to be cultivated, either with a horse and plow or with a hoe. Nick and Viola's horses helped with this task. A farmer's horses—or mules if he could afford them—were a major source of pride. A good horse could pull a plow through a tobacco field and never step on the tender plants. Horses could also be used to cultivate tobacco until it reached a certain height. After that they broke off the leaves as they walked between the rows, and farmers had to turn to hoes to chop out the weeds. It was exhausting labor, but tobacco growers were proud of their clean fields and often hoed them out several times, especially if they had enough child labor to do the work. In the summer of 1907, Nick and Viola's oldest son, Charlie, was eight and probably helped in the fields. But many more hands were required to hoe out five acres of weeds, and Nick probably hired neighbors, like the Coy boys who lived nearby.

Once the tobacco reached a certain stage of growth, weeds were less an issue than pests and diseases. A variety of diseases could affect a crop, including "blue mold, rust, wildfire, black shank, brown spot, root rot, and tobacco mosaic."[46] In most cases a farmer could control these problems only by careful field selection and pristine plant bed sites.

Numerous pests also affected the tobacco crop, but the worst was the tobacco worm. In Nick's day the only way to control worms was to walk the rows and pick them off and kill them, either by pinching them between fingers or stomping on them. Worming was also a job in which the whole family became involved. In the early 1900s, Paris Green, a highly toxic lead compound in the form of dust, was available commercially to control tobacco worms. Farmers could blow it onto the tobacco leaf, but it was very dangerous if they breathed it in or ingested it. Most used manual labor to control the worms.

When the plants finally became mature, they sprouted blooms on top of the stalks. In order for the plant to put all its energy into leaf growth, the blooms had to be topped, or broken off. Again topping was done by hand: farmers walked along the rows, breaking off the blooms. An unwanted result of topping was the appearance of new leaves, or suckers, on the stalk. Since farmers wanted all the growth to go into the existing leaves, they had to walk between the rows and break off the suckers as they formed. Usually topping and suckering occurred about a month before harvesting, in the hottest period of the summer.

And while Nick and other tobacco growers worked in their baking fields in the summer of 1907, the politics of pooling was also heating up.

CHAPTER FIVE

Glorious News

If only one name is remembered in Harrison County tobacco history, it is the name of Clarence LeBus. In the early 1900s, Clarence LeBus was famous, in Harrison County and beyond, as the champion of the poolers and the Burley Tobacco Society in the Bluegrass. As president of the BTS and the tobacco grower with the largest acreage in Harrison County, LeBus became the standard bearer for the right of the farmer to receive a fair price for his tobacco crop. From 1906 to 1910, he worked tirelessly to organize and unite farmers to stand together.

Born in December 1862, Clarence LeBus was the son of a wealthy landowner and farmer, Lewis LeBus. Lewis was a first-generation American, born and raised in Ohio, whose parents had immigrated to the United States in 1830 from Alsace, France. Clarence's father was a well-educated man who, early in his adult life, had taught school both in Ohio and Harrison County. The largest landowner in Harrison County, Lewis also had extensive holdings in Kentucky, Alabama, Ohio, and California. Clarence's mother was Martha Garnett, the "granddaughter of a noted pioneer Methodist minister Josiah Whitaker."[47]

With wealth and spiritual fervor in his lineage, Clarence LeBus started with advantages most men never had. Even so, as a young man, he did not wait idly to inherit his fortune. He apprenticed himself in various businesses, including in the tobacco business as a solicitor for the Bonman Warehouse Company of Cincinnati. By the age of thirty-five, he had acquired two thousand acres of land on his own and raised more tobacco with tenant farmers than any other producer in Harrison County.[48] He was a mature man in his forties when the tobacco wars between the ATC and BTS built to a climax. LeBus watched the iron grip of James Duke and the ATC tighten around the tobacco market in the first years of the twentieth century. He had more at stake in breaking that grip than any other man in Harrison County. And he rose to the task.

Where did he get the organizing skills? Even though his father was a schoolteacher for part of his life, Clarence did not complete college as a young man, "leaving college on account of weak eyes."[49] Nor did he appear to have had any earlier experience in politics. To understand how LeBus and the BTS managed to organize three-fourths of the tobacco growers, those same growers James Duke called "damn fool farmers," it is necessary to look back to the foundations on which he built. LeBus could not have prevailed without the earlier work of populist organizers in Kentucky, work begun by the American Society of Equity (ASE).

The ASE had been formed in 1902 by James A. Everitt of Indianapolis. Everitt, a rural retail merchant, understood the plight of family farmers. It was Everitt who first came up with the plan to pool the tobacco crop and to "meet one seller with one buyer."[50] While the ASE had no structural way of organizing farmers, it brought them face-to-face in conversation. From that beginning, local unions had formed in several Bluegrass counties by 1906. First these unions canvassed neighboring farmers on the idea of pooling; then representatives met together in New Castle, Kentucky, on October 1, 1906. They decided to organize as "the Burley Tobacco Society, A Branch Society of the American Society of Equity."[51] By January 1, 1907, twenty-nine counties were represented at a meeting in Winchester to decide whether the tobacco crop of 1907 should be pooled. Over 50 percent of farmers had to be in favor of the pool for it to go forward. The totals came to 54 percent, and the pool was on.[52]

When Clarence LeBus was elected president of the Burley Tobacco Society in December 1906, he was literally in the right place at the right time, the

moment when the pent-up frustration and desperation of individual farmers reached a peak. Although
LeBus did not appear to be a public speaker or
writer (most of the rhetoric quoted in local newspapers came from other leaders), he must have had
the force of character and personality to inspire
others to follow. He also had business savvy, which
helped him organize a financial structure to shore up
the poolers, who would have no income until their
pooled crop sold at some future date.

To that end, in early 1907 LeBus was instru-
mental in forming the Harrison County Tobacco
Company. He stated that the company was
formed "for the purpose of borrowing and loan-
ing money… for tobacco holders by going security
therefor [*sic*]; for warehousing, handling, grading
and prizing tobacco, in fact do any and all kinds
of business, and more especially looking after the
interests of tobacco holders".[53] The shares in the
company were to be ten dollars each, and twenty-
five thousand dollars had to be raised to finance
the undertaking. Initially LeBus and several other
leaders bought most of the shares. LeBus was confident, however, that in the long run the BTS would
make hundreds of thousands of dollars for growers
every year. And he also knew a good investment;
the Harrison County Tobacco Company would
become an essential service for many of the poolers. They would need a place to store their tobacco,
select grades, and prepare it for transportation to
the buyer. There was money to be made in all these

steps and the opportunity to get in on the ground floor of an enormous market.

Clarence LeBus's moment of greatest triumph came on November 19, 1908. After rallying farmers to pool their crops of 1906 and 1907 and hold the tobacco off the market to force a fair price from the American Tobacco Company, LeBus and other leaders pulled off the monumental task of convincing farmers to grow no crop in 1908, thus limiting the supply of tobacco available to the ATC at a time when its supplies were dwindling.

The gamble worked. Finally the ATC broke and purchased nearly the whole supply of pooled tobacco at prices dictated by the BTS. In a *Log Cabin* article under the headline "Glorious News for the Tobacco Farmer," LeBus phoned in the story from negotiations in Louisville: "We have closed deal with the ATC for 75% of the 1907 crop of pooled tobacco at the average price of 17 cents. Also, the remainder of the 1906 crop, at the graded prices, running from 18 cents to 30 cents per pound. Break the news to the faithful."[54] Following this success, newspapers idolized Clarence LeBus, describing him as a hero, the "Napoleon of the Burley district, a man of matchless business ability, sterling honesty, unswerving loyalty, dogged determination."[55]

In November of 1908, it appeared that the dream of the farmers to break the Trust was fulfilled and that an organization was now in place that would represent the farmers' economic interests far into the future. Though the dream would not prevail, in the fall of 1908 the BTS seemed invincible, and poolers had a season of glorious achievement. The Harrison County Tobacco Company and the BTS appeared to be victors over the Trust (ATC). Everything had converged for success: the ATC had run low on tobacco supplies, the pool had locked up most of the tobacco to be sold in the Bluegrass, and the government had indicted the ATC as an unlawful trust under the Sherman Antitrust Act.[56] Even though the ATC would appeal, it appeared the Trust would be broken into smaller companies and competition would once again exist in the market.

But all was not well in the pooling organization that had miraculously brought down the ATC. Discord and internal criticism had been building over the two years of its existence: Questions arose whether Clarence LeBus had sold some of his tobacco out of the pool and whether he had used his position to manipulate whose pooled tobacco would be sold. Farmers clamored to know what process was in place to assure their crop was picked for sale to a buyer. Some were angered by the fact that even when their crop was sold, 25 percent of the payment was held back until all the tobacco of that grade was sold, and then 10 percent was held back until the whole year's crop was sold, "to protect those parties whose tobacco has not been sold."[57]

Even as the cash began to flow back into local banks from the sale of nearly $12.5 million worth of tobacco, protests were heard.[58] On January 9, 1909, in a letter published by officers of the National Bank of Cynthiana, the Farmers National Bank, and the Cynthiana Bank, the bankers themselves protested the way in which the 10 percent deposit fee held by the BTS was paid back to the farmers. They complained that checks were being paid out in certain banks where the farmer was being "importuned to leave his deposit at said bank."[59] And farmers, who had waited nearly three years without income, complained about delays in getting paid for their crops.

To make matters worse, the executive committee of the BTS made a decision that added fuel to the farmers' concerns that some were profiting more than others from the pooling process. In June 1909 *The Cynthiana Democrat* newspaper reported that the committee awarded salaries to several officers, most notably to Clarence LeBus, offering "a salary of $12,000 for the past two years, and $15,000 for the ensuing year."[60] The executive committee assured poolers that "not a cent of this salary comes off the tobacco grower. It is paid out of the fee of $3 per hogshead which the buyers are required to pay." Nevertheless, the perception that selfish interests at the top were betraying a democratic movement was devastating.

The BTS also came into conflict with its partner organization, the American Society of Equity. In the days following the 1908 sale of more than twelve million dollars worth of tobacco, the ASE asked for funds to handle its operating expenses. The BTS refused and even denied a loan to the ASE to cover its expenses. Even though the ASE and BTS appeared to reconcile their differences in August of 1909 when the BTS paid "$10,000 to ASE to be divided equally between National and State unions for help in pooling the 1909 crop," the damage was done.[61] Rival pooling organizations began to spring up, undermining the already weakening resolve of farmers to pool their 1909 crop with the BTS.

The new pledge for the 1909 crop also included a clause that became a point of dissension and ultimately was fatal to the BTS. Printed in abbreviated form in the February 4 edition of the *Cynthiana Democrat*, the pledge omitted a controversial clause, which stated that farmers who pooled would automatically "subscribe for shares of the capitol stock, to the amount equal to 10 percent of the gross sales of the tobacco hereby pledged."[62] Once it became widely known that farmers would be required to pay 10 percent of their 1909 crop earnings to purchase shares in a new enterprise, one in which they had no input, sentiment swelled against pooling with the BTS.

Suddenly it was the fall of 1909, and the percentage of farmers who had signed the new pledge was dangerously low. The BTS called for an all-day meeting of growers on September 11 to rekindle enthusiasm. With the deadline of October 1 looming to vote the pool up or down, LeBus lectured farmers that "United assistance will mean success for years to come in this good county—without it we will have cheap labor, cheap land and everything else in proportion."[63] To ensure high attendance,

LeBus announced the BTS would hand out checks to pooling farmers for 8 percent of the 10 percent deposit held back on their earlier pooled crops. At the meeting several high-powered speakers and politicians gave long impassioned speeches on behalf of Clarence LeBus and the pool, including Kentucky Representative A.O. Stanley, Senator W.O. Bradley, and Justice E. C. O'Rear of the Kentucky Court of Appeals. Following the meeting LeBus and the BTS officers were so concerned that LeBus announced, "I here and now cheerfully waive my right to the ten thousand dollar bonus voted me by the district board June 9, 1909."[64] On October 7, the *Democrat* carried this headline: "Amount Pooled Equals 63%." Even so, the numbers of farmers who signed the 1909 pool were about one-third of those who had previously signed.

Matters would become even worse in 1910. On Court Day in Cynthiana, July 1, 1910, a vigorous debate took place among community leaders, including ministers, newspaper editors, and farmers. Clarence LeBus spoke up at this meeting, and his delivery was described as "sledgehammer jolts."[65] He declared "it was his intention to retire from the Presidency in the Fall but showed his faith in the permanent success of the society by publicly offering to take at par value all of the stock held in the Burley Tobacco Company, by reason of the 10% clause in the 1909 pool contract."[66]

With the 1909 pooled crop unsold, the American Tobacco Company took advantage of the controversies

by continuing to pay high prices to independent growers outside the pool. In some cases, the ATC bought
crops in the field at a stated rate, regardless of the condition in which these crops might be delivered.[67] Numerous lawsuits, some of them frivolous, were filed against
Clarence LeBus and the BTS. LeBus complained that
"suits aggregating nearly a million dollars have been
filed against me by enemies of this organization."[68]

By October 1909 the failure of the BTS was
clear. With less than 20 percent of the 1910 crop
declared for the BTS pool, *The Log Cabin* headline on October 21 proclaimed "1910 Burley Pool
Declared Off!" After meeting in extraordinary session, the BTS Executive Committee declared the
1910 pool off, based on reports that "trust buyers…
were flooding the country like a tidal wave, buying
crops without even inspecting the same." Clarence
LeBus again spoke out at this meeting, insisting "that
we are forced to back track but only to get a stronger
foothold."[69]

But the reality was different. By the end of
December 1910, total tobacco sales of over four million pounds in Lexington averaged $9.09 per one
hundred pounds, nearly six cents less than the price
the ATC paid for the 1906–1907 pooled crops. The
BTS was not able to regroup, nor did any newer
cooperatives attract large numbers of farmers. Prices
continued to fluctuate and trend downward, keeping farmers in the grip of banks and buyers for the
next generation. The ATC was found in violation
of the Sherman Antitrust Act in 1911 and forced

into dissolution but reorganized into several smaller companies, still owned by the same shareholders, which simply carved up the tobacco market to avoid competition.[70]

Not until the federal government stepped in during the Great Depression did the tobacco market begin to stabilize and provide predictable income for farmers. The government pool finally accomplished the goal of Clarence LeBus and the farmers who pooled their tobacco in 1907. After nearly thirty more years of an unpredictable market for farmers, the US government intervened and stabilized production with the Agricultural Adjustment Act (AAA) in 1933. This act "set up acreage restrictions on tobacco [and] provided a government-supported loan program to farmers against surplus production."[71] Other legislation evolved, establishing tobacco allotments on farms currently raising tobacco and prohibiting farmers who had not previously established a tobacco base from raising tobacco. The government, through the mechanism of the Agricultural Stabilization and Conservation Service, monitored and controlled the amount of tobacco a farmer could produce, first by limiting acreage and later by limiting poundage.[72] The result, finally, was a stable market that limited supply to meet demand and guaranteed a minimum price for the crop.

Unlike most tobacco farmers in the early 1900s, Clarence LeBus died a wealthy man. In 1928 his obituary reports that he owned thirty-eight thousand acres of farmlands in seven counties as well as several businesses and was a major shareholder in several banks.[73] But ultimately he was unsuccessful in the greatest challenge of his life—the challenge of maintaining the trust of tobacco farmers in the BTS and forcing the ATC to pay a fair price.

CHAPTER SIX

Women's World

While the world of Harrison County men was increasingly dominated by tobacco politics, women in the early 1900s had varying priorities. Newspaper articles about local women range from frivolous activities to sobering obituaries; they yield a snapshot of the times in which Viola Muntz lived.

Most newspaper accounts of women's activities were related to church and community news. Under "Local News Briefs," a variety of information was reported, such as "Miss Flora Martin took the first premium on fancy work at the Falmouth Fair last week."[74] Women were also often involved in fund-raising events for good causes. The Presbyterian Aid Society in Cynthiana sponsored a sale of "water-color pictures, fancy calendars, candies, etc.,"[75] and "the ladies of the Baptist church…[held] their Thanksgiving cake sale next door to the post office."[76] The November 29, 1907, paper noted that "the ladies of the W.C.T.U. [Women's Christian Temperance Union] will hold another window sale" to fight the abuses of alcohol. They were apparently successful, even to the point that they managed to close the saloons in Cynthiana in early 1908.

Women in rural areas, more spread out and isolated, had fewer opportunities to congregate. Articles sent in to the newspaper carried news of Harrison County rural communities (Headquarters, Berry, Connersville, Renaker, Oddville, Sylvan Dell, Sunrise and so on) reporting the births, deaths, illnesses, and social activities of families and churches in the outlying areas. From Headquarters, the paper reported that "Miss Rainey Smith has been very ill with the lagrippe the past week."[77] In the same edition, the Oddville news reported that "Gladys, the bright little daughter of Mr. and Mrs. George Toadvine, is much improved after several weeks of illness." From Sunrise came the all too common sad news that "the infant child of Luther Perkins that died last Friday near Leesburg was buried at Sunrise Saturday." There was even a note about one of Viola and Nick's children in the Oddville news: "Miss Alice Muntz, of near Sylvan Dell, has been visiting relatives in this community." Alice, eight years old, was probably visiting her grandfather, Joseph Muntz Jr., and her step-grandmother, Lizzie Benson Muntz.

Occasionally enthusiastic accounts appeared of parties and meetings in homes, such as the news from Leesburg in February 1909, when "Mrs. H.H. Chinn entertained the Book Club Wednesday last… The program, being one to commemorate St. Valentine, was well carried out under the able direction of the hostess, and it is reported by the attendees to be one of the best meetings of the club." In the same edition, there appeared an extravagant report of a George Washington birthday party at the home of Miss Myra Paul: "The house was decorated with flags and bunting…The hostess wore a costume and appeared to superb advantage…and never was assembled a brighter or happier group of young people."[78]

One fascinating news story involved, of all things, a popularity contest. Its contestants were women from throughout Harrison County. In a story titled "Getting Lively," on April 17, 1908, *The Log Cabin* reported on a very competitive popularity contest created as a clever marketing tool by the paper. All ballots had to be clipped from *The Log Cabin* and sent in by a deadline. The number of ballots received proved that the event was hotly contested. "Mrs. J.D. Swinford, who has held first place from the opening of the contest, passed into second place this week, being led by Miss Stella Turner by 350 votes….A new entry this week is Miss Della Brunker of Sylvan Dell, and she makes a fine start with 790." The newspaper reported voting in several Cynthiana districts, as well as Oddville, Sylvan Dell, Lair,

Leesburg, Connersville, Cason, Kinman, Berry, Colemansville, and Claysville; and the leading lady, Miss Stella Turner, was reported to have 8,280 votes. One month later Mrs. Perry Phillips of District B pulled ahead with 12,665 votes![79] By the spring of 1908, Viola Muntz had five children, ages nine, eight, five, three, and eight months. Her name did not appear as a contestant in the popularity contest.

Another intriguing news story, from Louisville, Kentucky, was carried in *The Log Cabin* in 1908. It involved a young woman who disguised herself as a boy to work on a riverboat. "Birdie Helms, aged 16 years, has always dressed in man's attire in her positions as…barkeeper, porter and cabin boy."[80] Apparently she was discovered by juvenile authorities, who sent her to a girls' school "attired in her proper vestments as a girl…rustling taffeta and shiny heeled shoes." Within three weeks she ran away and was caught again, "dressed to a suspender button in the very clothes she wore as a 'cabin boy.'" The article did not chronicle Birdie's fate after being arrested the second time. But apparently not every young woman accepted being relegated to the role of the weaker sex.

Women of the social elite, even in tiny Cynthiana, enjoyed the privilege of higher education. The *Log Cabin* "Personal and Social" column of June 14, 1907, reported that Miss Agnes Ball Smith graduated from Vassar College on June 12 and that her mother, Mrs. Lizzie Smith, attended the commencement exercises. Another young woman, Miss Carrie

Fitzwater, was described on March 22, 1907, "as one of Cynthiana's talented musicians" who had completed her musical education in a Cincinnati college. A popular Cincinnati composer, Mr. C.S. Morrison, dedicated a new piano solo, "Flower Song," to Miss Fitzwater. An all-female college also existed at that time, in Millersburg, Kentucky, located in Bourbon County, just next-door to Harrison. Millersburg Female College was described in *The Log Cabin* as "one of the oldest institutions of learning in the South."[81] This college was one of hundreds established by the Methodist Church throughout the country. Destroyed by fire on October 9, 1907, it was rebuilt and eventually became a part of Millersburg Military Institute.[82]

Not every young woman respected the privilege of higher education, as evidenced by a report on June 1, 1906, in *The Log Cabin*. A certain Miss Sadie Margaret McGinnis was denied her diploma from Campbell-Hagerman College in Lexington, Kentucky, because she "repeatedly violated the rules regarding dancing...Notwithstanding...repeated warnings...the young woman continued to attend hops and other amusements and dance with the young men." Miss McGinnis sued the college and the faculty for denying her degree. The outcome of her suit was not reported.

At the turn of the century, most Harrison County women did not attend college. Viola Judy could have been the exception, because her family was relatively prosperous and she did not marry Nick until she was twenty-three years old. At that time Harrison County had numerous county schools, grades one through twelve, and she probably attended the one nearest her home, Buena Vista School, in the Salem District. It is described in the *History of Bourbon, Scott, Harrison, and Nicholas Counties, Kentucky,* published in 1882, when Viola was seven years old. "The school is an excellent one, and has a daily attendance of about sixty pupils. It has been in charge of Prof. J. Florence for about three years, who has brought it to a good state of perfection."[83] Viola may have met Nick at school. Census records for 1895 to 1897 show that Nick attended school in the Salem District.[84] Although Viola would have graduated by then, they may have first become acquainted with each other in earlier years.

Although there was no hint in newspapers of the role women played in raising and housing tobacco in the early 1900s, they almost surely helped at various times of the growing season: planting, hoeing, and worming tobacco fields. The poorer the family, the more likely that women and children would help in these tasks. Women who cared about their reputations in the early 1900s, however, preferred to pretend that they had no knowledge of or involvement in raising tobacco.[85] Viola Muntz probably did not help out in the tobacco fields for the obvious reason that she was pregnant or nursing during most of the years she and Nick were married. Sometime around 1908 she contracted typhoid fever, a terrible disease from which she never fully recovered. Even so, she would have performed all the support tasks for those working in the fields, providing hot meals for harvesters in the fall and cold food for the strippers in the stripping room in the late fall and winter. Her health would not have excused her from the necessity of this work.

Local stories and obituaries in *The Log Cabin* reported the precarious health system of the period and the sometimes grisly treatments. On July 20, 1906, the paper described the resetting of Shirley Frisbie's broken arm: "The ends of the broken arm were sawed off and...were fastened together with silver wire. It is believed that the bone thus held together will knit together rapidly." Obituaries catalogued the common diseases that killed people in the early twentieth century, diseases that hardly exist today. Under "Deaths" on April 19, 1907, *The Log Cabin* reported, "Mrs. Mary Renaker, aged 69 years old...died of measles." And further, "Mrs. Lafe Beagle...died of typhoid fever on Tuesday afternoon... The death is a sad one, as she was in the prime of life, being 34 years of age and has three young children to lose a mother's care."

Compared to the lack of information about most women, one woman's name appeared with tantalizing regularity in stories related to the Burley Tobacco Society: Miss Alice Lloyd. Alice Lloyd was mentioned in news stories regarding the BTS from 1907 to 1910. She apparently served as secretary to Clarence LeBus and press secretary for the Burley Tobacco Society, at least in Harrison County. A natural assumption would identify her as the same Alice Lloyd who became an educational reformer in Appalachia around 1916 and ultimately established more than a hundred public schools in that region. But the facts contradict that assumption. According to P. David Searles in *A College for Appalachia,* Alice Lloyd, whose maiden name was Alice Geddes, did not marry Arthur Lloyd until February 1914. She did not move from Boston to Knott County, Kentucky, until the summer of 1915.[86]

The Alice Lloyd associated with the Burley Tobacco Society had to be a different person. Who was she? Although no biographical information was reported about her in the local newspapers, the accounts of her activities showed her to be an educated and outspoken woman, one confident enough to make fiery speeches in public settings dominated by men.

By September of 1909, the BTS had achieved significant success against the American Tobacco Company. The BTS entered 1909 in a position of strength, but it was not without detractors. One bone of contention was the notorious "10 percent clause," which the BTS buried in the body of the new pledge that farmers were required to sign to pool their tobacco.[87]

Many speeches and public debates arose out of the 10 percent clause. Notable public figures spoke at these public forums, such as Clarence LeBus and A.L. Ferguson of the BTS; M.C. Rankin, state commissioner of agriculture; W.P. Kimball, ex-congressman from Ashland; Colonel Cassius M. Clay, Jr.; and Campbell Cantrill of the American Society of Equity.[88] In the midst of these orators, according to newspaper articles, Miss Alice Lloyd also stood up and attacked opponents' arguments and was greeted with great enthusiasm. On September 2, 1909, *The Cynthiana Democrat* reported, "Miss Lloyd delivered an eloquent talk upon the higher aims of the movement; what its success meant to the whole state— to education, to charities, to public institutions, to churches, to homes, to comfort and culture." Quoting her actual words, the article further stated: "When the tobacco grower, the man whose crop is Kentucky's mainstay, gets a fair price for his product there will be money in the treasury. Then when we need a library or money for a church or a school we will not have to go east and ask millionaires." According to the newspaper, she was received with wild applause.

A strong debater, Lloyd dealt her opponents on the platform some humiliating blows. On her response to a speech by M.F. Sharpe of the ASE opposing the 10 percent pledge, the *Democrat* reported:

> He was rather severe in his criticisms, but suffered more severely at the hands of Miss Alice Lloyd, who replied to his address and gave him a decidedly uncomfortable half hour. Her thrusts at the discomfited organizer caught the fancy of the audiences, and furnished a great

amount of amusement. Her questions were so embarrassing that Mr. Sharp in desperation appealed to the audience to know whether it was the province of a press representative to ask questions and answer speeches. Miss Lloyd replied that it was the duty of press representatives to condemn error and refute falsehood wherever found.[89]

Even so, Miss Lloyd's most famous debating opponent was Colonel Cassius M. Clay Jr. Clay was the son of the noted abolitionist Cassius Marcellus Clay and came from a long tradition of public service and politics. Like his father, he was not afraid to oppose popular issues. Clay Jr. was an opponent of tobacco pooling in general and the Burley Tobacco Society in particular. He was obviously not a proponent of women's rights, especially when that woman was Alice Lloyd. Clay complained at length of her attacks on him in a speech he made in Paris, Kentucky, on August 2: "In that speech I did not refer to Miss Lloyd at all. I, not like Miss Lloyd, have a good many other things to do besides writing for the press and, consequently, will make this article as brief as possible."[90] This statement by Clay was followed by a lengthy point-by-point refutation of Alice Lloyd's criticisms, which suggested that he took her remarks seriously. Whatever Lloyd's status, she got the attention of men in positions of influence. She also obviously had the ability to excite and sway an audience.

Lloyd's involvement in the BTS continued at least into 1910, when she traveled to Washington to testify on behalf of the BTS on the question of whether it had violated the Sherman Antitrust Act. Lloyd was a member of a committee including an attorney, John R. Allen; Commissioner of Agriculture H.M. Rankin; and Honorable C.C. Patrick. In an interview after returning from Washington, Lloyd spoke for the committee: "My conclusion drawn from… evidence in the hands of the department of Justice is that the Burley Tobacco Society will not be proceeded against by the Federal government or that if further investigation is made…the only effect will be to make the Burley Tobacco Society stronger and to prove it guiltless of many charges that have been brought against it by its enemies."[91]

In spite of Lloyd's passionate defense, the BTS would lose the faith of the farmers who pooled their tobacco and all but disappear in the next two years. As did Alice Lloyd. Her name is not mentioned in any of the research about the period, except in the daily accounts in the local newspapers. Although she and Viola Judy were very different women, they share the fact that they have been forgotten by history, at least until now.

CHAPTER SEVEN

Night Riders

One of the most shameful chapters in the tobacco wars involved the night riders, shadowy masked figures who rode out in darkness and committed violence against property and people who chose not to pool tobacco. As early as 1906, stories began to circulate in *The Log Cabin* about distant violence associated with tobacco growers.

Several years before the Bluegrass Region of Kentucky organized against James Duke and the American Tobacco Company, the Black Patch movement sprang up in southwestern Kentucky and north-central Tennessee. The Black Patch organization, the Planters Protective Association, was created at a meeting in Guthrie, Kentucky, on September 24, 1904. Even at the height of its popularity, the

PPA enlisted only about one-third of the growers in its cause. As early as 1905, certain desperate elements within the organization turned to violence to convince farmers to pool their tobacco. There is evidence that the PPA leadership, while publicly denouncing violence, tacitly sympathized with it as a means to an end.[92] The infamous night riders, vigilante groups that threatened and destroyed both lives and property, became a fixture of the countryside.

Black Patch tobacco, or dark tobacco, is very different from burley. In *The Politics of Despair*, Tracy Campbell describes Black Patch tobacco: "The soil of the western regions of the two states was particularly suited for a dark, strong-flavored variety of tobacco, used primarily in the manufacture of snuff, chewing tobacco, and cigars."[93] The dark tobacco reflected the early consuming habits of customers and lacked the adaptability of the burley leaf for various kinds of products. Since much of their tobacco was purchased for export, growers of black patch tobacco were even more vulnerable to the vagaries of the marketplace than burley growers.

Between 1906 and 1909, *The Log Cabin* reported an escalating stream of violent events in the Black Patch region. In the "Kentucky News" column on May 25, 1906, the paper included a paragraph about Hopkinsville, Kentucky, titled "Destroying Tobacco Beds." "The tobacco plant bed containing 450 square yards, on the farm of L.L. Leavill, was visited by unknown parties and destroyed. Mr. Leavill is not a member of the Dark Tobacco Planters' Protective association and says threats have been made against his plant beds." On May 31, 1907, *The Log Cabin* reported an incident in Princeton, Kentucky: "At midnight 35 masked men went to the home of Noble Robinson…and, after firing several volleys, ordered him to come out.…Robinson was then forced to go with the men to his tobacco bed and participate in its destruction."

The troubles involved much more than tobacco beds. On November 8, 1907, *The Log Cabin* stated, "Night riders burned two houses on the farm of Mr. Hendrix, in Trigg County, after forcing him to leave his home…One of the houses was occupied and the tenants were forced to leave and remove their furniture, after which the torch was applied." Large organized teams of night riders also attacked warehouses and barns full of tobacco sold to so-called independent buyers who were actually agents of the American Tobacco Company, even though their companies may have had local names.

The most sensational event occurred in Hopkinsville, Kentucky, on December 7, 1907. According to *The Log Cabin,*

> Five hundred "night riders," masked and heavily armed, marched into Hopkinsville at 2 o'clock this morning and destroyed property valued at over $200,000.…The police, Fire Department, telephone and telegraph offices and even the railroad stations were in possession of

> a wild mob shooting right and left....The
> action of the "night riders" in going after
> not only the tobacco warehouses of the
> town, but seeking as well to injure other
> property, is a new turn in the trend of
> affairs.

Not long after that event, the newly elected governor of the state, Augustus E. Willson, called out the state militia to restore order.

Soon reports of vigilante groups in the Bluegrass Region of Kentucky also began to creep into the pages of *The Log Cabin*. Incidents in Bath, Nicholas, and Shelby counties were reported in late 1907. By that time, the Burley Tobacco Society in Harrison County had pooled two years of crops but failed to sell them to the ATC for the price they demanded. The hardship and anxiety of the last two years were beginning to take their toll in this area as well.

On top of that, the BTS proposed no crop for 1908. At a large tobacco meeting at the Cynthiana courthouse on November 9, 1907, a number of speakers harangued the audience about signing the pledge to grow no crop in the upcoming season. Judge J.J. Osborne voiced the mood of the crowd:

> At the outset he declared that every
> grower should make a special effort to
> prevent lawlessness in any form, and that
> even if they could get 40 cents per pound
> for tobacco it would not compensate them

for a state of lawlessness in the Blue Grass. He said this was a free country and men could not be driven. But on the contrary, he declared that every patriotic grower ought to stand by the majority of his fellows. He said true patriotism meant to stand for the greatest good for the greatest number. He said that it was an undisputed fact that those in the pool had made the increased price for those out of the pool and the patriotic, neighborly thing for those who had reaped the benefit was to sign the pledge of no crop next year.[94]

From 1907 on, stories of panics about rumors of night riders and sightings of night riders became common in the Bluegrass Region. Mounted police were called out in Lexington on December 10 to guard warehouses holding tobacco raised by independent growers. The growers themselves also helped to guard the houses, but no night riders appeared.[95] More often, the night riders visited isolated growers, where they had the advantage of surprise and numbers. At times they even became day riders, intercepting independent growers on their way to market with loads of tobacco, threatening, turning over wagons, and forcing their owners to turn around.[96]

In the midst of all this tension, the BTS denounced the violence in a resolution published in *The Log Cabin*: "We are opposed to unlawful invasion and violation of law, both by corporations and individuals, and pledge ourselves to aid in the prosecution of those guilty thereof."[97] Yet at other gatherings of the BTS, speakers protested angrily against both the ATC and the independent growers. One speaker managed to build a position on the logic that night riders had a right to attack independents because the independents were aiding and abetting the Trust.

Governor Willson, realizing that things were getting out of hand, proposed a tobacco summit. He called the growers and the buyers to meet together in Frankfort on December 20 and 21, 1907. His plan was "to hear their grievance and the facts upon which they are based.…He believes…he will be able to bring together, upon a basis of just and honorable understanding, these representatives so that the tobacco now on hand will find a fair market at satisfactory prices, and that the buyers will be satisfied with the adjustment."[98] Clarence LeBus and many other county BTS representatives attended. James Duke did not. He sent his general manager, Mr. R.K. Smith, who was authorized to sign contracts but not to negotiate price. Duke's highest offer was twelve cents a pound. The BTS's lowest selling price was fifteen cents a pound. And there the deal stuck. Duke refused another meeting, and the pressure for no crop in 1908 was on.

The threats and night rider violence continued to grow. In March 1908 Henry Ellis, an independent grower in Henry County, was visited by night riders who took him prisoner and set fire to his house.[99]

Later that same March, in Nicholas County, an independent farmer named Hiram Hedges paid the ultimate price for growing tobacco. He was shot and killed standing in his own doorway. According to his wife, the family was awakened in the middle of the night by voices shouting and demanding that Hedges come out. He started to the door with his gun, but Mrs. Hedges convinced him to leave the gun and go to the door unarmed. Hedges pleaded with the men to leave and even promised he would destroy his tobacco bed the next morning, but one of the riders shot Hedges in the stomach with a shotgun. He died before a doctor could arrive. Hiram Hedges left behind a wife and six children.[100]

In Covington during the same week, night riders burned an enormous warehouse filled with independent tobacco. "Five houses, one and two-story brick dwellings, adjoining the warehouse were burned, the occupants, mostly white families, barely escaping with their lives, so rapidly did the fire spread."[101] Miraculously the fire was contained before it spread throughout the city.

The night rider vigilantes also created a climate and a cover for shadowy violence of all sorts. A Shelby County farmer, Newton B. Hazelett, was found dead of a shotgun wound in late May 1908. First reports indicated he was a night rider who had been shot by a farmer protecting his barn. Other reports assert he was assassinated because "there had been bad blood between his family and another family in the neighborhood."[102] In Maysville, "A band of 15 men called

Samuel Rigdon from his house and beat him with whips until blood ran down his body."[103] Ironically Rigdon had already pooled his tobacco crop.

Protected by masks and anonymity, night riders sometimes used their power against African-American farmers, suggesting that racial hatred was an element in these events. One such incident occurred near Hickman, Kentucky, in the Black Patch area in October 1908. "Dave Walker, a negro, his five-year-old daughter and his baby were killed outright, the mother who was holding the baby in her arms, was fatally shot, and three other children will probably die as a result of the mob's visit to the Walker home." The supposed offense was that "Walker had cursed a white woman and threatened a white man with a pistol."[104] For that accusation, a whole family was brutally murdered by night riders. Two things become apparent in all these stories: there were numerous bands of night riders spread over a wide geographic area, and these bands were increasingly vicious toward those with whom they disagreed.

The extent of the acceptance of this violence can be seen in letters and speeches quoted in *The Log Cabin*. With specious logic one writer, who signed his letter "An American Citizen In spirit as well as Name," managed to blame the unfortunate Hiram Hedges for his own murder, because as a non-pooler Hedges forced the night riders to attack him: "Hiram Hedges…gave to organized resistance to the trust the heaviest single blow it has had in the Burley belt;

he put one more rivet in the shackles the trust seems to fasten upon the people."[105]

Surprisingly, until 1908, there was little or no physical violence in Harrison County, although many angry words were spoken and printed. In contrast to the highly reported opinions of the poolers, the independent growers remained silent. The Judy family appeared to have been united as independents. But neighbors all around them had pooled their tobacco, so there must have been tension on Judy Ridge Road. Even Nick's father, Joseph Muntz, was likely to have been sympathetic to the BTS and poolers. Joseph was a member of the "Fair Play Grange," and Granges in general were populist organizations dedicated to the collective good of their agrarian members. Was there also tension between Nick and his own family about growing tobacco? Nick and Viola were associated with the Republican Church on Republican Pike. Did they attend church and find that neighbors shunned their pew? Was it just German and Swedish stubbornness that made them suspicious about giving control of their tobacco crops to the BTS? Was it the ever-increasing number of children who needed to be fed and clothed? These questions have no simple answers.

CHAPTER EIGHT

Burned Out

Near midnight on December 7, 1909, night riders visited Ed Judy's barn near Beaver Baptist. Filled with five thousand pounds of stripped tobacco, the barn was an ideal target. At least three men skulked up to the outbuilding and threw in the torches that flamed up hungrily. The barn was soon a roaring inferno that crackled out the tall, narrow side-vent doors and through the roof.[106]

Ed's farm was next door to Viola and Nick's homestead and adjacent to younger brother James's farm. James first saw the flames and ran toward his own barn to free the livestock in case his barn was next. Several shots rang out in his direction, but the riders galloped off. Only Ed's barn burned down, but the loss was complete. Ed had just sold his tobacco crop to a Cynthiana buyer named Edward Bahr for thirteen cents a pound, but had not yet had a chance to deliver it. His crop was not pooled, nor was James's or Nick's. Had they not been scared off, the night riders might have set all the barns on fire.

The destruction of Ed Judy's property was apparently the first barn burning in Harrison County, and it occurred much later than most. But a pattern of violence had been building around Harrison County. Out of thirty-four local newspaper accounts of night riders and state militia response in 1908, eighteen occurred in Harrison County and the counties that bordered Harrison (Bracken, Robertson, Nicholas, Bourbon, Scott, Grant, and Pendleton).

Earlier persuasive efforts had been mainly peaceful. On November 1, 1907, *The Log Cabin* reported that a tobacco buyer, Mr. William Blackburn, was visited by a group of about twenty-five tobacco growers who came to ask that he cease buying unpooled tobacco. Blackburn stated, "When the men started away they said they hoped another visit would not be necessary and suggested they might be a little more emphatic next time." Other buyers throughout the Bluegrass Region received visits with similar demands. Stories appeared about "night walkers" who walked alongside wagons on their way to market to discourage the sellers, and about the "Peace Army," small groups of men who canvassed neighborhoods to persuade their neighbors to join the BTS pool.[107]

In early 1908, representatives of the Peace Army visited the Sylvan Dell precinct, where Nick and Viola lived. They reported that "they had pledges to cut out the 1908 crop, representing 316 acres out of a possible total of 450 acres…there are only seven or eight men in Sylvan Dell precinct who have refused to agree to cut out the next crop."[108] Nick Muntz and members of the Judy family were some of those men; the division in the Sylvan Dell area was clear early on.

Efforts to persuade independents soon became more chilling. Tacked onto B.F. Whitaker's barn in Sunrise was this note: "If you receive any tobacco in this barn we will blow it to Hell, and you with it!"[109] In Nicholas County at Upper Blue Licks, the threats became reality on February 21, 1908. A tobacco barn belonging to Aubrey Smoot, "a farmer and independent tobacco buyer," was burned by arsonists.[110] In Bracken County in March a hundred masked men "burned 20,000 pounds of tobacco belonging to H.L. Staton, an independent buyer."[111] Tobacco beds were burned near Leesburg.[112] The violence was edging closer.

In 1908 the state militia came to Harrison County. When Governor Willson called out the militia to deal with the terrible violence in Hopkinsville, as well as other areas of the state, a local company of militiamen set up quarters in Cynthiana. The Cynthiana militia withdrew near the end of January. *The Log Cabin* reported their lack of success sarcastically: "they repelled every onslaught of the night riders, without loss on either side."[113]

The local sheriff and militia were again called into play in May when about forty night riders from Bracken and Robertson counties waylaid three wagons of tobacco on their way to Lexington for sale outside the pool. One wagon was turned over, and the drivers were forced to turn back with the rest. The following week the Cynthiana sheriff sent the local militia to escort the wagons, and they arrived safely in Cynthiana and then traveled on to Lexington.[114] The state militia divided into bands and patrolled the Bluegrass Region in an attempt to deter any further lawlessness. Since the militia never knew where or when the night riders might attack, their efforts were largely futile.

Like the militia, the justice system was also largely ineffective. Because of fear, rarely would anyone testify against perpetrators of violence. If victims did testify, objective jurors could not be found. The incident in 1908, involving the masked day riders who turned back three wagons in Bracken County loaded with non-pooled tobacco, did come to trial. The court had difficulty providing a list of potential jurors. When the jurors were selected, the prosecution had difficulty with its witnesses. They "thought they recognized [but]…would not be positive. [One]…"was scared. On cross-examination [he] said masks covered all of men's heads."[115] All the defendants were found not guilty.

Local independents began to be alarmed, and some were reported to have taken vigilante action of their own in response. They banded together and went out at night shooting their guns. "The shooting was done by six or seven independent farmers of near Leesburg who say they will grow tobacco. They had heard talk of raiders coming from Scott County to visit them. They got together, bought some shells at Leesburg and fired a number of volleys to try their guns."[116]

Throughout 1908 *The Log Cabin* carried various articles that superficially condemned violence but suggested the independents deserved what they got. The newspaper ran a full letter on March 13 signed by "A Converted Independent" that stated, "If he [the independent] persists in his right to grow a crop this year, he will bring about one of two things; either defeat the object of the Society to raise the price of tobacco, or he invites acts of lawlessness on the part of the more violent and unreflecting element in the community." Another letter appeared from a "repentant Independent" who had received a threatening letter: "In the still watches of last night the scales of custom, inertia, stubborn individualism, prejudice, preconception, selfishness, fell from my eyes and I fully determined before your note was received to announce my conversion at the earliest possible moment."[117]

In that same edition, the newspaper noted that "35 night riders in Bracken [C]ounty severely whipped Henry Gross and George Gross because they were arranging to raise tobacco." On May 22 *The Log Cabin* reported night riders visited a farm in Scott County near the Harrison County line and scraped and destroyed twelve tobacco beds. A load of tobacco owned by A.J. Aulick was overturned and the wagon destroyed in July just over the Pendleton line. Anonymous poolers in the area were quoted as stating, "Mr. Aulick had his meat house, and barns well filled and plenty to live on, and could join the pool as well as some of those who were living on cornbread and blackberries."[118] With the 1907 crop still sitting in BTS warehouses and no crop in 1908, the poolers were low on tolerance.

As the summer progressed, heat and drought added to the tensions. Poolers who grew no tobacco planted replacement crops to bring in income and food. But they were thwarted even in those efforts. "From June 11 to November 10 central Kentucky endured the worst drought since the establishment of weather records in 1871."[119] Small ponds and streams literally disappeared. The tobacco crop was also affected. According to *The Log Cabin* on November 6, 1908, "the crop of 1908 was cut beyond our most sanguine expectations and the great drouth [*sic*] has still further diminished the available supply."[120] Independents like Nick Muntz and the Judys would suffer as well, but that was small comfort to the poolers. Everyone who farmed, no matter what the crop, suffered.

But that was 1908, before the Burley Tobacco Society pulled off its greatest triumph over the American Tobacco Company, forcing the Duke enterprise to buy the pooled crops of 1906 and 1907 at the price set by the BTS. The 1909 *Cynthiana*

Democrat and *Log Cabin* carried almost no accounts of night riders and violence during the year, even though there had been many accounts in 1908. And in 1909, in the wake of mistrust of its officers, the BTS was struggling to enlist enough farmers even to pool the 1909 crop. The sentiment for pooling was barely lukewarm among smaller farmers and tenants since a higher proportion of their crops' value would be paid back to the BTS in handling fees and mandatory purchase of shares in the Harrison Tobacco Company. Historians generally agree that the influence of the night riders died out in 1909 because "the cooperative tobacco organizations within the state had disintegrated and the riders quickly disappeared."[121] So why was Ed Judy's barn burned down in December 1909? The timing of the event seemed out of rhythm with the momentum of the night riders around the state.

It may have been pure revenge. A strong cadre of poolers lived in the Sylvan Dell area of Harrison County along Judy Ridge Road near Nick and Viola and her brothers. As early as 1906, Herbert Wyles, D.E. McCauley, and J.M. Florence acted as precinct canvassers to enlist their neighbors to sign the pooling contract. Ironically, Herbert Wyles and John Milt Florence were involved in the tragic events that followed three nights after Ed Judy's barn burned. Perhaps these men were secretly gratified that Ed Judy's crop went up in flames. There is no evidence, however, that any of them were involved in the barn burning.

Whoever the night riders were, they knew the neighborhood and the independents. They may have come across the line from Bracken or Robertson County, where violence had occurred routinely over the last three years. Whether they were neighbors or not, they were probably known to the neighbors who had been loyal to the pool. These same neighbors had watched the Judys and Nick Muntz plant and harvest crops in 1906 and 1907 that were sold to the ATC, crops that put food on the table and clothes on the backs of their families when everyone else was sacrificing. Driving up and down Judy Ridge Road, they watched the independents plant a crop in 1908 when the BTS had pledged its members to plant no tobacco and limit the supply available to James Duke and the ATC. Maybe, as the saying goes, it still stuck in their craw. The barn burning on December 7, 1909, was vindication.

CHAPTER NINE

Shot Down

When the sun came up on Wednesday, December 8, Ed Judy's barn and its contents were reduced to a smoldering ruin. Ed, his brother James, and Nick likely congregated on the site and sullenly watched the dying embers. Fear and resentment began to grow in the men. A whole year's work, from burning seedbeds to planting to weeding to topping and suckering, from cutting and hauling to housing, and finally, the stripping! Two months, standing in the cold barn stripping and tying hands, had come down to this, down to nothing. And there were bills to be paid, goods bought on notes, on promises, promises that must be kept when the crop sold. And now it was gone.

The Judys and the Muntzes were not joiners. They were not visionaries. They didn't get involved in politics. They took care of their families and helped each other and asked no outsiders to help them survive. They worked hard, knowing that weather and natural disaster could undermine any man, no matter how productive he was. They never would have considered it another man's fault if their crop failed or they didn't get the price they wanted. They would never have carried a torch and burned a neighbor's livelihood to the ground. But now they realized the price of independence.

Nick had to be thinking about what such a disaster would mean to him and Viola. After a poor crop in 1908, they needed the income from this year's crop to balance out their accounts. Five children— Charlie, Alice, Rose, Ray, and Kenneth—were bursting the house at the seams, and Viola was due again in February. On top of that, Viola's health was a growing concern. Since contracting typhoid fever, she had suffered relapses that made her weak, with reoccurring bouts of confusion and even delirium. When these relapses came on, she was hardly able to function, and her state of mind alarmed both Nick and the children. Nick had to hire a neighbor, Mrs. Taylor, to come in when these bouts occurred. What was to become of them all?

Something hardened in Nick's mind after the fire, and on Wednesday morning he decided to go to town and buy a gun. He went alone, and it is not clear why Ed and James didn't join him. Perhaps they already had guns to protect their homes, even though their guns had not helped due to the element of surprise. Nick believed he had to be prepared for another surprise attack. He bought a rifle and returned home.

On Wednesday afternoon Sheriff Gragg came out from Cynthiana to examine the crime scene. He probably asked questions about the value of the crop and what the men had seen and heard and then turned around and went back to town. After all, the likelihood of finding and prosecuting the perpetrators was slim. The night riders struck and fled and left little evidence behind. And the neighbors weren't talking.

By Thursday, December 9, Nick and Ed had examined all their worries about the return of the night riders, turning the matter over and over. The two men determined they must do something, and they decided to go to Cynthiana and send a telegram to Governor Willson asking for protection by the state militia.

But they still found time that day to help a neighbor. Thursday morning young neighbor Elva Coy came by and asked to borrow Nick's team and wagon to haul a load of turkeys to the stockyards and pick up some provisions. Later, telling his story to the *Cynthiana Democrat*, Nick "said that he and young Coy were friends and that Coy had frequently been employed by him in stripping tobacco and other work about the farm."[122] The newspaper stated that Elva was about twenty-three years old and that he "was the chief support of his widowed mother, who with two younger sons resides about a half-mile from the home of Nick Muntz." In contrast, federal census records show that there were five children in the Coy family: the oldest son was Robert J., about twenty-six in 1910; a sister, Ella, twenty-one; Elva, about nineteen; and two other brothers, John William, nineteen, and Irvin, fifteen.[123] Elva was either a twin of John William or they were born within the same year.

Elva's brothers, Robert, John Bill, and Irvin were probably with him that morning. Nick helped them load the wagon and then rode part of the way with them into town while Ed followed in a buggy. Apparently Nick switched to Ed's buggy close to town, and they followed the boys to the stockyards, where they unloaded the turkeys. They then accompanied the boys to a local grocer, perhaps W.B. Rouse or Milner's, where they loaded up flour and provisions for the Coy family. By that time it was close to dusk, and the boys started for home in the wagon.

The printed account in the *Democrat* of Nick's actions on Wednesday and Thursday was silent about the timing of the rest of the day's events. It did not detail when Nick and Ed telegraphed Governor Willson. Did they stop and do that as soon as they arrived in town? Or did they get involved with the Coy brothers' needs and postpone the telegram until late in the afternoon? The *Democrat* only reported, "While in Cynthiana, Muntz and Judy tried to communicate with Gov. Willson in an effort to secure protection for themselves and others of the neighborhood who had tobacco which had not been pooled, and which they thought was in danger of being destroyed. They received no response from Gov. Willson."[124]

Another action taken by Nick was even more confusing. "Wednesday morning Muntz came to Cynthiana and bought a rifle and some ammunition. He brought the rifle back, Thursday, and exchanged it for a shotgun."[125] Why would Nick trade the rifle in for a shotgun? Was the rifle too expensive? Was Nick a poor marksman who decided a shotgun would be a more practical weapon for scaring away marauders? He later testified that he was "unaccustomed to handling weapons." Did he shy away from the deadliness of a rifle, preferring a more scattershot gun? Whatever the reason and timing of their actions, Nick and Ed were extremely concerned about a return of the night riders, and they had little confidence in receiving any help from the local authorities.

Although not mentioned in Nick's account of the events of Thursday, apparently Nick and Ed also found some alcohol that afternoon or evening. How they got access to liquor is a mystery, since the growing Temperance movement had closed the saloons in Cynthiana in 1908. On this cold December afternoon, Nick and Ed managed to find a place to buy a warming liquid (unless they had brought it from home). Perhaps the grocer where the Coys bought their provisions had an illegal backroom business. However they did it, the *Cynthiana Democrat* reported, "Muntz is said to have been drinking in Cynthiana Thursday afternoon."

By the time Nick and Ed started for home that evening, it was dark. This was nearly the shortest day of the year, so it would have been after 5:30 p.m. The distance from Nick and Ed's homesteads on Judy Ridge Road to Cynthiana was nearly twelve miles, and traveling by horse and buggy was probably about a two-hour trip. The *Democrat* described the events that occurred as they drove home alone. "It is reported that as he [Nick] and Ed. [*sic*] Judy drove along the pike in their neighborhood, several shots were fired from the buggy." Based on testimony at the examining trial, Nick and Ed were enthusiastically testing the new shotgun. Several neighbors described the shots they heard on Thursday night. "Harry Shields testified that on the night of the shooting he heard two shots fired near his gate as a buggy passed. Two others were fired near Dow McCauley's and two near Hub Wyles' home." These two neighbors were poolers and had canvassed the Sylvan Dell precinct earlier, trying to persuade tobacco growers around them to pool their crops as well.

What actually happened in the buggy on the long ride home? Ed Judy's testimony at the examining trial offered one explanation:

> Ed. Judy told of his coming to town with Nick Muntz Thursday, that Muntz got a shot gun at Hamon's and said he was going to defend his barn. Muntz took two or three drinks while on the way home with him in the buggy, but was not drunk.

He, Judy, suggested that they fire the gun as they went along to make the people believe the night riders were after them again. The gun was fired several times.[126]

Perhaps Nick and Ed, influenced by several swallows of whiskey, decided to shoot in the air as they passed by their pooler neighbors just to throw a scare into them. Whatever the reason, they foolishly demonstrated their presence and condition all up and down the road.

When Nick stepped out of the buggy at the end of his lane, sometime between 8:00 and 9:00 p.m., he was suddenly alone in the dark with a shotgun. In his own words quoted in the *Democrat,* Nick said,

> I was nervous and excited…on account of the burning of the barn and through fear of night riders. As I was approaching my gate, a man came running toward me out of the darkness. I called to him and asked who he was. He didn't answer, but kept coming towards me. I called again, and even a third time, but got no reply. Then I fired. I missed him. I fired again, and this time he exclaimed, "My God, you have killed me."

The nightmare had begun. Nick stated later that he "did not know whom he had shot," but in his frenzy of trying to unbreech and reload the shotgun, he expected "night riders to charge upon him…he tried to unbreach [*sic*] his gun and load again, but could not 'break' the gun." In the awful ecstasy of the moment, Nick couldn't reload the gun, even though he had reloaded it several times when firing into the air earlier.

Nick ran, in the opposite direction from the dreadfully familiar voice that had screamed out to him. Again the newspaper account was contradictory. It stated that he ran first to neighbor John Milt Florence's house, but it later stated that Nick went to Ed Judy's house, which seemed more likely. Judy testified that "Muntz came to his home about nine o'clock, greatly excited and told of shooting a man, didn't know whom. Judy sent his sons to investigate." Apparently Nick went to Florence's house next, for John Milt Florence had a telephone. In the examining trial, he described how an anguished Nick Muntz knocked on his door in the middle of the evening and cried out that he had shot someone, perhaps one of the Coy boys. For the first time, Nick put into words his terrible fear that he had shot a friend and neighbor. Florence, with Nick, "at once started to find the wounded man, but was met by young Judy and asked to telephone for a doctor, which he did. Afterwards he and Muntz met Hub Wyles and others taking young Coy home in a buggy." Now was the moment which Nick could no longer postpone, the moment when he came face-to-face with the man he had shot, and it was not John Bill Coy. It was Elva Coy, the young man who had borrowed his team just that morning, the young neighbor he had helped in town with his chores, the son of Minnie Coy whom Nick had called his friend.

Elva Coy lived until about 4:00 a.m. on Friday, December 10. Before he died, he told his story, which was later reported at the examining trial. Elva said that he had been at Nick's barn in the dark because he was returning his team and wagon. He was in a hurry to get home because of all the excitement in the neighborhood. He apparently said that:

> Muntz did not call to him and the first that he knew of his presence was when the first shot was fired. He said the report of the gun frightened him badly and he was sure night riders were trying to kill him. He ran all the faster towards his home, which carried him towards Muntz. Then the second shot was fired and he received a fatal wound.[127]

Dr. W.D. Stewart, who was by Elva's side at his death, would give conflicting testimony at the examining trial regarding Coy's last words. He reported that Coy told him Nick did call out three times but Coy was too afraid to respond. Unfortunately, his testimony would not soften the community's judgment of Nick.

What must it have been like in the home of Nick and Viola Muntz later that evening? How could Nick open the door, enter the house, and tell his wife, seven months pregnant and weakened by typhoid fever, that he had killed their neighbor and friend? The nightmare now began to engulf both Nick and Viola.

CHAPTER TEN

Consequences

Whatever transpired late Thursday evening between Nick and Viola, Friday morning still came, along with the awful reality of Thursday's events. On this morning Nick decided to go back into Cynthiana and surrender himself to the authorities for shooting and killing Elva Coy. A summary of events in the *Cynthiana Democrat* reported, "he came to Cynthiana with his father and friends and was put in jail."[128] Nick surrendered himself to Sheriff Gragg and made application for bail. The application was denied by the presiding judge, in advance of an examining trial, and Nick went to jail. The order of events following that moment is confusing in the newspaper account, but apparently Nick turned to lawyers for help only after this bail was denied. Since he was in jail, someone else would have had to hire lawyers on his behalf, probably his father, Joseph.

Realizing the gravity of Nick's situation, Joseph turned to the attorneys he had probably used for various legal matters over the years, the firm of J.J. Osborne and M.C. Swinford. The Swinford name was well established in 1910 and is still a legend today in Harrison County. M.C. Swinford, a self-made man, read law under Judge J.Q. Ward and was admitted to the bar in 1879. Over the years he served as county school superintendent, county attorney, and Harrison County representative.[129] Joseph Muntz chose the man he thought most able to help Nick navigate the legal system.

On that same Friday, December 10, the Coroner J.W. Smiser "held an inquest over the remains of Coy."[130] This medical inquest involved a jury. Even though Dr. Smiser did not make public the verdict of the jury, the *Democrat* reported that "the jury found the killing unjustifiable."

Knowing the political hard feeling against independent tobacco growers, M.C. Swinford had to realize this would be a hard case. Just how hard would become clear with the charge brought against Nick on the following Monday.

The funeral and burial of Elva Coy took place on Saturday, December 11. He was buried in Beaver Baptist Cemetery in Harrison County. Elva died less than a year after his father, leaving his mother and brothers alone to scrape out a living on the farm. Soon Viola would also be left to raise six children alone. A shot, fired in terror, had tragic consequences for two women and eleven children in two families and reverberated in the lives of their descendants for generations.

That same Saturday morning, M.C. Swinford and J.J. Osborne appeared before Judge J.E. King, the presiding judge of the Harrison County Court, and offered a motion to place Nick Muntz in the custody of the sheriff until Thursday. Nick was already in jail in the sheriff's custody, but the newspaper account offered no explanation of this motion. Perhaps it would have allowed Nick to go free, required only to report to the sheriff. Judge King denied the motion but set an examining trial for Monday, December 13. The prisoner was sent back to jail. Nick spent three days and three nights in the Cynthiana jail with nothing to do except revisit the events of the previous Thursday.

Over that time he must also have been a prisoner of his emotions, alternately wracked by anger, fear, denial, horror, shame, remorse. Questions without answers must have run through his head over and over:

Why did Elva have to be coming out the lane at precisely the moment I arrived home?

Why didn't Elva call out his name when I called to him? Elva was my friend and neighbor; I would never have fired if I'd known it was Elva.

Why didn't I stay away from alcohol so that my mind was clearer?

Weren't the real killers the night riders, the cowardly men who burned and destroyed other people's lives?

What would happen to Viola, and Charlie and Alice and Rose and Ray and Kenneth? And the baby not yet born?

By the time Monday morning came around, Nick had to be a different man, burdened with the full mantle of responsibility for what he had done, no matter how he wished he could undo it.

Monday, December 13, was a day of great excitement in Cynthiana. According to the *Democrat*, the examining trial was set for 10:00 a.m. in the circuit court room. This trial was actually a preliminary examining trial conducted by the Harrison County Court, but it had all the excitement of opening day for circuit court.

The county seat courtroom in those days was the setting for tense debate, high drama, and even entertainment. In his memoir, *Kentucky Lawyer*, Judge Mac Swinford (son of M.C. Swinford) quoted an observer describing a typical court day:

> Monday morning the court room is packed, hitching space along the horse racks, erected on three sides of the courthouse, is at a premium, for every able-bodied man in the county came to the opening of the circuit court in those days. The assemblage in the courthouse is tense as the judge opens his court, empanels his juries and instructs the Grand Jury. Those instructions were eagerly listened to by the people, and was [*sic*] an event in their lives and their conversation thereafter.[131]

True to form the *Democrat* stated that on Monday, December 13, the "circuit court room was crowded with spectators."[132] Judge J.E. King presided. Commonwealth Attorney Dedman and County Attorneys M.G. Land and Wade H. Lail represented the state. J.J. Osborne and M.C. Swinford stood for the defense. Family members and neighbors were present, as undoubtedly were many curious onlookers who wanted a glimpse of the unfortunate Nick Muntz, the independent tobacco grower who had not joined the pool and now had killed his young neighbor thinking he was a night rider.

Judge King informed the defendant of the charge of willful murder against him. Nick entered a plea of not guilty. The court had issued two sets of summons on December 11 for various witnesses to appear. For the defense, "Ed Judy, James Judy, Minnie Judy, John Milt Florence, Roy Muntz, Charles Wilson, and Frank Muntz" were summoned. For the state, "Tate Shields, Dow McCauley, Joe Mathers, Willie Jenkins, Hub Wyles, Luther Mastin, and Ed Judy and J.M. Florence" were summoned. [133] Ed Judy and J.M. Florence were called by both sides. All appeared that day with the exception of Minnie Judy and Will Jenkins, "not found" by Sheriff Gragg. Except for Nick and Viola's relatives, all were neighbors who lived on Judy Ridge or Beaver Baptist Road. The official court documents provided no detail of the testimonies, stating simply that "The parries [*sic*] then announced ready for trial, and after hearing the evidence and the Court being sufficiently advised, has reasonable grounds to believe the defendant guilty."[134]

The newspaper account, on the other hand, embellished the details, though the details were often contradictory. The first to testify was Dr. W.D. Stewart, the physician who treated the dying Elva Coy. Dr. Stewart testified that "Coy said to him Muntz had called on him to halt three times before he was shot, but that he did not stop because he was scared." In another part of the same story, the *Democrat* reported that Elva Coy never heard a voice call out, that "the first he knew of his [Nick's] presence was when the first shot was fired."[135] The two contradictory accounts were never reconciled.

John Milt Florence, a neighbor and a friend, "told of Muntz coming to his house Thursday night, much excited and crying; said he had shot an innocent boy, didn't know who, but was afraid it was John Bill Coy." Why didn't Nick investigate after he knew he had shot someone? Why, if he had the slightest suspicion that it was a friend, didn't he run toward him and try to give him comfort? Those are questions that were not answered or even asked in the report of the examining trial.

Another neighbor, Harry "Tate" Shields, testified "on the night of the shooting he heard two shots fired near his gate as a buggy passed." Shields had obviously conducted his own investigation, since he reported he found "empty shells the next morning, and some wads marked for No. 4 shot, on the pike near his home." Neighbor Hub Wyles testified that

"Boss Garrison came for him on Thursday night and they found Elva Coy lying on the road. He got his buggy and took the wounded boy home." How did Wyles and Garrison know someone had been shot? How did they know where to go to find the body? And why was Boss Garrison not summoned to testify? None of these questions are answered in the testimony.

Finally the *Democrat* detailed the testimony of Ed Judy, Nick's brother-in-law and the man closest to him all day Thursday. Judy was a sympathetic witness for Nick and even cast blame on himself for some of the events leading up to the shooting. He reported that Nick "got a shotgun at Hamon's and said he was going to defend his barn." Ed stated that "Muntz took two or three drinks while on the way home in a buggy, but was not drunk. He, Judy, suggested that they fire the gun as they went along to make the people believe the night riders were after them again." Judy's testimony suggested the events leading up to the shooting were simply a prank played by two fellows who had a few drinks. He further testified that he "didn't hear any shooting after Muntz got out of the buggy." Considering he had just dropped Nick off when Nick encountered Elva Coy coming home, it is hard to imagine he heard nothing and had no idea what had happened until "Muntz came to his home about nine o'clock, greatly excited and told of shooting a man, didn't know whom." At that moment "Judy sent his sons to investigate." Perhaps Ed Judy was more inebriated than he admitted.

The testimonies of the witnesses raised several questions that were not answered. Obviously numerous men were out on Judy Ridge Road on Thursday evening. At times they seemed to know more than they could possibly know in the dark during the hours the tragedy played out. Perhaps several of them had phones and talked to each other. Clearly John Milt Florence had a phone, for he called the doctor. The court didn't worry about the details because this was an examining trial and none of these men were on trial. Nick Muntz was.

The official affidavit read that "Nicholas Muntz did unlawfully, feloniously, willfully and with malice aforethought kill and murder Elva Coy by shooting him with a gun loaded with powder and ball or other hard substance from which shooting the said Coy did die...."[136] The charge against Nick Muntz was "Wilful murder." The court asked for a warrant of arrest. The judge's summary of court proceedings stated that Nick "be held to answer and [*sic*] indictment that may be found against him by the Grand Jury in session at the February term 1910 of the Harrison Circuit Court growing out of the said charge described in the affidavit filed herein against him."[137]

Since the circuit court did not meet until the fourth Monday in February, Judge King allowed bail "in the sum of $10,000 for his appearance in said Court for the purpose above stated." This seemed to be a staggering amount of money for the time, but somehow Nick raised bail. He still had friends and family who stood up for him. Those who gave sureties for his bail bond were "D.N. Rees, J.E. Hayes, J.W. Stump, Gano Ammerman, Joe Muntz, Chas. S. Ewing and J.T. [probably J.F.] McCauley."[138]

Six of these seven men were listed in the 1910 federal census. Joe Muntz, of course, was Nick's father. Joseph Hayes was Nick's nephew, son of Lina Muntz, Nick's half-sister, and Ewing Hayes. D.N. Rees, J.W. Stump, Chas. Ewing, and J.F. McCauley were not relatives. J.F. McCauley lived on Salem Pike, a neighbor of Joseph Muntz. The other three men all had Cynthiana addresses. In an ironic side note, J.W. Stump lived on Pike Street, the same street as Clarence LeBus, the leader of the tobacco pooling BTS. Curiously, no member of the Judy family gave surety for Nick's bail bond.

And then Nick went home. Events in his life from that day on were a downward spiral. Far from taking responsibility for his wife and children, Nick suffered a mental breakdown, and he required care. The *Cynthiana Democrat* stated, "Muntz's mind became shattered and he was taken to a sanitarium in Lexington for treatment. In addition to the killing of Coy he had been laboring under mental distress on account of sickness in his family, business reverses, and a seeming train of misfortune."[139] Probably his father, Joseph, again stepped up and saw to it that Nick was placed where he could be protected from himself.

The newspaper account was unclear on the length of time Nick stayed in the sanitarium, but he returned to Cynthiana on Thursday, February 10. A heavy snow fell that day, making the roads nearly impassable. "On account of the heavy snow…and the bad condition of the roads, he was not taken to his own home, but spent the night with one of his brothers. Friday morning he went home."

A neighbor, Mrs. Taylor, was at Nick and Viola's that day, helping out as a nurse to Viola. She was probably Birdie Taylor, another neighbor of Joseph Muntz. The newspaper accounts never mentioned the children. Were they at home or had they been sent to relatives until Viola's health improved? Hopefully none of them witnessed the events of that afternoon. According to the *Democrat*, Nick "appeared restless and uneasy, and Mrs. Taylor…kept a close watch on him. Finally it was suggested that he be allowed to go out on the farm and get some exercise if he desired. He was gone perhaps thirty minutes before his family became alarmed."

That Friday afternoon when Nick walked out to the barn, the snow made his passage difficult, but he persevered. Once he was inside, the total despair of his situation must have settled upon him.

He…secured a large linked trace chain and made a running noose with the ring on the end of the chain. This he placed around his neck and fastened the other end to the beam which extended over the driveway. Then he either jumped or fell off the beam. The ring in the chain caught him under the chin, and the jar broke his neck. He probably died instantly.[140]

And then, with a precious attention to detail, the *Democrat* reported: "There was scarcely an abrasion of the skin, the chain having been placed under the soft collar of his shirt."

Mrs. Taylor found him. She searched several places before looking in the barn. "Then, peering through a crack in the partly closed door she saw Muntz's body dangling from a crossbeam, about midway of the driveway." When she realized he was lifeless, she began screaming for help. A nearby neighbor, George Duckworth, ran to help and took the body down. The *Democrat* summed it up: "Thus ends a chapter of a wretched and deplorable state of affairs."

Unraveling

The unraveling of Nick and Viola's family had begun, and events now moved swiftly. Nick's funeral was held two days after his suicide, on Sunday, February 13, 1910. He was buried in the Republican Church cemetery in Buena Vista, just off the Republican Pike and a few miles from his home.[141] The little log church, on a ridge overlooking a valley, must have seemed the loneliest place in the world that day. Deep snow, the same snow that had prevented Nick from traveling home earlier in the week, blanketed the frozen ground, creating a challenge to mourners and gravediggers.

The service was probably small due to the circumstances of Nick's death. Perhaps even Viola was absent, since she was so ill and close to full term in her pregnancy. The children may have been present, under the care of relatives. Charlie, the oldest, was almost eleven; Alice was nearly ten; Rose, just seven; Ray, four; and Kenneth, two years old. Or they may have been kept away, protected from the awful truth by caregivers. Almost surely the Muntz family was in full attendance: father, Joseph, and step-mother, Lizzie; brothers Louis, Roy, Walter, and half-brother Elbert; sister, Laura, and half-sister, Lina. The Judys were probably represented by Viola's brothers, Ed, James, and Virgil, and some members from the maternal Pope side of the family. All told, probably no more than about twenty mourners were present unless a few neighbors attended. And when it was over, everyone went home to face the cold reality of February.

Two days later, on February 15, Nick's father, Joseph, came to Cynthiana and petitioned the Harrison County Court for administration of Nick's estate. Joseph told the court that:

> Viola Muntz, the widow of Geo. [George] N. Muntz is of weak and feeble mind and has been in that condition mentally since she had typhoid fever in the summer and fall of 1908. That her mind is so weak and imbecile that she is because of that condition incapacitated from administering upon the personal estate of her husband.[142]

The court granted Joseph's petition and made him administrator of the estate.

Joseph wasted no time. Two days later, with the court-appointed appraisers, he conducted an appraisal of the worth of Nick's personal estate. The meager property "not exempt from distribution" was catalogued:

Cash on Hand	485.90
6 Hogs	65.00
1 Wagon	25.00
1 Buggy	5.00
2 Pr work harness	5.00
1 Culling Harrow	15.00
1 Dirt Scoop	2.00
½ Interest Cutter Plow	2.00
3 Plows	5.00
1 A Harrow & Dray	1.00
1 Saddle	2.00
Lot Corn in Crib	40.00
Hog	10.00
Sledge Hammer, Crowbar & Pick	2.00
Lot Meat	50.00
Lard	5.00
	$719.90[143]

Other estate items, mostly farm implements and food, were appraised and set aside for the widow. The total value of those items was $769. One of the listed items simply stated, "in lieu of provision for six, $300."[144] Probably the six were Viola and her five children. Does this mean that someone else had already taken over Viola's duties? Perhaps that explained why Joseph Muntz acted so quickly in appraising Nick's estate.

Two days later, on February 19, 1910, Viola gave birth to the youngest and last child from her marriage to Nick: infant Clara Muntz. Her husband was dead; her health in shambles; five other children needed parents; and here was a newborn baby. Even so, perhaps Clara brought her a moment's comfort, presenting the demands of a new life in the midst of death and despair.

With all the challenges, Viola's household was still intact in April, 1910, when the federal census taker stopped in. The census report stated that Viola was head of the household, white, thirty-five years old, widowed, and mother of six children, all living. The census also showed that Viola's occupation was farmer and that she owned her farm free of mortgage.[145]

On February 6, 1911, almost a year after Nick's death, Joseph Muntz filed the final settlement of Nick's estate with the Harrison County Court.[146] He detailed payments of $485.97 to settle various debts to retailers, such as VanHook Hardware and Crescent Milling Company, as well as the coroner and Whaley's Funeral Home. Two bills were notable because they shed light on the last days of Nick and Viola. One large bill for $90 was settled with the sanitarium where Joseph placed Nick to protect him in the weeks before his death. The other, for $17.50, was paid to Mrs. M. J. Taylor for nursing services to Viola, and perhaps for baby Clara. When all debts were settled, a sum of $186.70 was paid to Viola Muntz.

But Viola probably took little note of the final settlement of Nick's estate. Her health worsened, and she was placed in the Eastern Kentucky Asylum in Lexington, where she died after a few weeks, on April 3, 1911. Her death certificate stated that cause of death was "exhaustion following acute mania."[147] The contributory factor was listed as typhoid fever. The brief obituary in *The Log Cabin* stated that she was survived by six children.[148] After funeral services on April 5, Viola was buried in the Republican churchyard next to her husband.

On April 10 Viola's brother Virgil was granted administration of her estate, together with Nick's father, Joseph. The court appointed George Whitaker, John Milt Florence, and Robert Florence (all landowners and neighbors of Viola and Nick), to assist as appraisers.[149] John Milt Florence had helped rescue Elva Coy on the fateful night of December 9, 1909; he had been called as witness in Nick's examining trial both for the state and for the defendant, and now he was called to appraise the estate of Viola.

Virgil Judy and Joseph Muntz presented an Inventory and Appraisement of Viola Judy's personal estate to the court on April 18, valued at $1,461.71.[150] Even more poignant than Nick's, this inventory documents the unraveling of a farm, a household, and ultimately a family:

Property
Cash on Hand $11.76
Bank Acct   579.46

Notes
C.E. Judy   208.69
C.E. Judy   206.87
Travis Judy   167.50
J.T. McCauley, Jr.   18.25
J.C Henry   23.66
C.E. Judy   16.15
Virgil Judy   17.62
Joshua Florence   12.00

One mare   75.00
Pr. Work harness   3.00
One wagon   20.00
One stove   1.00
6 Beds and bedding   26.00
35 yds. Carpet   2.00
6 chairs   3.00
1 rocking chair   1.00
7 chairs   2.00
1 trunk   1.00
Bowl and pitcher   .50
1 clock   50
1 Washstand   2.00
1 Bureau   1.00
1 sewing machine   3.00
1 shot gun   6.00
1 safe and dishes   4.00
1 rag carpet   1.50
1 yarn carpet   1.00
1 silk quilt   3.00
2 thousands [*sic*]   6.00
5 locust Post   1.25
Lot of posts   1.00
Lot of tobacco sticks   15.00
800 lbs. of flour   20.00
Total Amt of Appraisements $1,461.71

On May 12, 1911, a Public Auction disposed of the personal estate of Viola Judy Muntz. The amount of money raised was only $148.77.[151] The final settlement of Viola's estate would not be completed until April 1913.

In May 1911 the countryside was erupting into spring. The struggle between the American Tobacco Company and the Kentucky Burley Society was over. The Supreme Court ruled that Duke's ATC had violated the Sherman Antitrust Act and required the dissolution of the ATC into three smaller companies. Ironically these companies were still controlled by the same owners and continued to cooperate to control the tobacco market.[152] The BTS pool was dissolved, dumping the 1909 pool of tobacco on the market, and once again it was every grower for himself. Five years of sacrifice and strife came to an end, and the economy of Harrison County settled back into subsistence. The children of Nick and Viola were about to be separated and taken into several households over a three-state area. The Judys and the Muntzes would resume their lives and bury the memory of this terrible chapter in their family histories.

CHAPTER TWELVE

Descendants

Though legal documents cannot sum up a person's life, they do demonstrate a family closing ranks to make the best of a tragic situation. Property had to be liquidated, debts had to be paid, and children had to be protected. The Muntz and Judy families had their hands full.

The final settlement of Viola Muntz's estate was recorded on April 9, 1913, with the Harrison County Court.[153] This document listed twenty-nine payments received from relatives and neighbors for various notes and for use of Viola's land for pasture and crops such as tobacco and corn. The value of these notes was not listed individually but appeared to be $546.94 based on other data in the settlement. The paid-out items, including doctor and funeral expenses, estate settlement costs, and labor, came to $1,255.32. One of the paid laborers was John Bill Coy, brother of Elva. The balance of cash left was $924.79, which was divided equally among the children. Each received $154.13, except for Clara, who received $144.14 after child care services were subtracted. Three additional notes, due in twelve months and worth a total of about $900, were included in the settlement. C.E. Judy, the same "Ed" who was the companion of Nick Muntz on that fateful December trip to Cynthiana, acted as guardian for the children. No mention was made in the final settlement of Viola's real estate holdings.

All of Viola's property was accounted for, however, in Harrison County Circuit Court records of 1916 and 1917. Ed Judy petitioned the court as plaintiff with all the children in 1916 for permission to sell Viola's homestead, the 47.34 acres where the family home and barn stood.[154] The court records included a deposition from Joseph Muntz in which he stated "it would be unreasonable" to divide the land up into six little tracts, especially since the tract with the house and barn would be worth more than any other tract. Joseph further speculated that the land "is good land. I would say [worth] $50.00 an acre....I think it would be decidedly the best now to sell."[155]

As a result the court held a public auction on the steps of the courthouse on September 25, 1916. The highest bidder was Ed Judy, who purchased the land for nearly $71 an acre, to be paid in a series of notes over time at an interest rate of 6 percent. The various guardians of the children (Joseph Muntz, Ed Judy, Virgil Judy, Roy Muntz, Frank Muntz, and William Morgan) signed bonds assuring that all monies received would go to the children. The property stayed in the Judy family, and the children received a generous settlement.

The only other court document that shed any light on property inherited by the six children of Viola Muntz was filed in Harrison Circuit Court on March 13, 1917, four years later. It related to the ownership of another parcel of land, inherited by Viola from her uncle A.J. Pope. Pope's will, made in 1907, stated that:

> My land or my Real Estate I give to my sister Rachel Pope as long as she lives at her death to be sold and especially divided between C. Ed Judy, Virgil Judy, Jim Judy and Viola Muntz heirs of James Judy dec'd, and Asa Pope and W.B. Pope heirs of W. Hade Pope. [156]

Viola inherited one-sixth of the 73.14-acre estate, or about 12 acres, sometime before 1910. Apparently the six children or their guardians believed the land was still owned by Viola. Ed Judy produced a deed of sale in court showing that Viola and all the other heirs sold their portions of the inheritance to him on March 4, 1910, for $1,962.50 apiece.[157] This sale occurred less than a month after Nick committed suicide and Clara was born. The court ruled that Ed Judy was the rightful owner of the land.

Beyond this incident there was no evidence of any ill will between the Muntz and Judy families. Joseph Muntz Jr. and Ed Judy worked together to achieve final settlements of Nick and Viola's estates. When Joseph died in 1920, Ed Judy served as one of his pallbearers. Only one act of omission, not commission, suggested that the Judy family seemed ready to turn away from the Muntzes. None of the Judy brothers in Harrison County took in any of the six children. The children were separated, and some were sent to live in distant households out of state. Nick and Viola's descendants would grow up apart, hardly knowing each other.

Charlie, the oldest, was twelve years old when his mother died. Born March 22, 1899, he was old enough to understand the events of the previous two years better than the other children but too young to take charge of the family. With the few assets controlled by guardian Ed Judy, Charlie had no vote. He and the other children would be separated. Apparently Charlie and his brother Kenneth went to the home of their uncle, Roy Muntz, in Harrison County sometime after Viola's death in 1911. Roy was Nick's older brother.

The only picture of Charlie (sometimes spelled Charley) Muntz is an undated family portrait of the

Roy Muntz family. One of six people in the portrait, Charlie is a young man. The images are identified as "Uncle Roy Muntz, Aunt Ruth, Clay Doan, Doan, Kenneth Muntz, and Charley Muntz." All five males wear coats and ties. Roy Muntz's son Doan and Ruth's nephew Clay Doan are wearing bow ties, while Roy's nephews Charlie and Kenneth are wearing long ties. Charlie is a handsome young man with a shock of brown hair pasted across his forehead and a bemused expression on his face. He is the only person in the portrait who has a hint of a smile.

ROY MUNTZ FAMILY

What was he thinking as he sat for that portrait? Was he proud to be counted a family member? Was he amused to be included, since his Uncle Roy identified him as a "boarder" in the 1920 federal census?[158] Eloise Judy (wife of Viola's nephew Edgar Judy), interviewed in 2009, shared the stories she had heard about Nick and Viola's family.[159] She remembered that Charlie "went to live with people he worked for." Even though Charlie moved in with his paternal uncle, the relationship may have been less than familial.

Probably the best luck in Charlie's life was meeting Mollie Jenkins and marrying her on July 3, 1929. By all accounts, Mollie was a loving and courageous woman. Over the next ten years, they had six children, five of whom survived: Blanche, born in 1930, followed by Eloise in 1933, Lenvil in 1935, Larry in 1939, and Janie in 1940.

Charlie Muntz worked most of his life as a farm laborer, doing the work he learned from his father. His only surviving child, Janie Muntz Kearns, recollects that "Daddy left by lantern and came home by lantern. He worked for L&N Railroad, and on farms, on thrashing machines."[160] Since she was not quite six when her father went away, her memories are minimal. Charlie died, at the young age of forty-seven, on January 20, 1947, after a twenty-one-month stay at Eastern State Hospital. Janie remembers that "Daddy had five hundred dollars worth of insurance. It bought a tombstone and a funeral." His death certificate shows that Charlie died of tuberculosis but lists as a contributing factor "Manic Depressive Psychosis, Depressed Type."[161]

Mollie held the family together after Charlie's death. According to Eloise Judy (wife of Viola's nephew), Viola Judy's brothers came forward to support Mollie and the children. Eloise remembers that Mollie "kept them [the children] together, worked and took in washing. Every year the three [Judy] brothers took money up to her; they killed hogs and took her meat, and a load of coal."

Janie's memories are similar. "Momma was determined that the family should stay united. Louis and Minnie Judy wanted to take Linville and Eloise [Janie's siblings] to live with them. Momma said, 'No, as long as we have a biscuit to share, we'll stay together.'" And Mollie worked heroically to provide. "Momma got forty dollars a month of welfare. She did laundry, cleaned houses, worked at the school lunchroom in Buena Vista and Oddville. She brought home food, peach juice, bread heels, for the kids. She also worked at Crook's Restaurant in Cynthiana." Even so, the toll of raising a family alone was great. Mollie died on August 25, 1954, when Janie was fourteen years old. Her death certificate cites "Coronary Failure" as the cause, but Janie remembers that Mollie died of an aneurism. Like a grim shadow, the cycle of separation followed Charlie and Mollie's family. Blanche and Eloise, the oldest, already had their own homes. Blanche took in Lenvil and Larry; Janie went to Midway to Pinkerton High School, a female orphans' high school, for four years.

Those children would grow up, marry, and bring nine grandchildren into the community of Harrison County. As of the last count, the grandchildren have brought fourteen great-grandchildren into the world. The descendants of Charlie and Mollie are still close, both geographically and as a family. They created a book of the Charlie Muntz family genealogy together in 2007.

Alice, Nick and Viola's second child, was born on April 2, 1900. At the time the children were separated she was eleven years old. The early accounts of what happened to Alice are vague. According to Eloise Judy (wife of Viola's nephew), "one of the girls" was sent to live with a Judy relative, Luttie Ragland, in Ohio.[162] Luttie was probably Viola's half-sister, Lou Ann, daughter of Elizabeth Ragland, the first wife of Viola's father, James.[163] Although Eloise wasn't sure which girl went to Luttie, Alice seems to be the best candidate. Both Rosa and Clara, her younger sisters, were sent out of state as well, but neither of them returned to live in Harrison County. Only Alice is in Harrison County as a young woman. According to Eloise, the girl who went to live with Luttie was very homesick and so distraught that Luttie sent her back to Harrison County. Alice appears in the 1920 federal census in the Harrison County home of Joseph Muntz, her grandfather.[164]

Another story comes from the memory of Mary Catherine Ritchie, Alice's only child. Mary Catherine has no knowledge of the circumstances surrounding the deaths of her grandparents, Viola and Nick. She knows only that their children were separated: "After the parents died, the kids were split up and Alice went to live with her grandpa. She went to work for and lived with the Charles Woods family—but [Mary Catherine] doesn't know at what age. She [Alice] was with them until she married Walker Wilson April 16, 1924."[165] Walker Wilson's full name was Walker Woods Wilson; perhaps he was related to the Woods family that employed Alice. At some point she and Walker moved to Covington, Kentucky, where they lived the rest of their lives. Walker was a railroad supervisor in Covington. Their only child, Mary Catherine, was born on February 19, 1925.

Two photos exist of Alice. Both are undated, but the first, probably taken around 1920, is a portrait of a young woman. The only word on the photo is "Aunt," printed in the bottom right-hand corner, but that title could have been added at a later date. Probably the picture was taken around the time of her marriage to Walker. Looking straight into the camera, Alice has a perfect oval face with large dark eyes. Her hair is also very dark and pulled back away from her face, probably into a bun. She wears no jewelry, but her dress has a flattering wide crossed-sash collar. Alice's mouth is composed with the suggestion of a smile. Together the features create the face of a beautiful young woman, one who embraces her future.

PORTRAIT OF ALICE MUNTZ WILSON

The second picture, a snapshot of Alice and Walker probably taken in the 1960s, is outside, perhaps in their yard. Alice's niece Janie Muntz Kearns, who shared this picture, remembers Alice as a kind and jolly person. Here, many years later, Alice and Walker are seniors with graying hair and thickening figures. It is an equally beautiful picture filled with affection. On the left, Walker has his right arm around Alice. In her arms she holds a small dog. Both Walker and Alice are smiling. Alice's face is reminiscent of her brother, my grandfather Ray. The stocky German heritage imposes itself on her in maturity as it did on his figure.

ALICE MUNTZ WILSON AND WARREN WILSON

Alice and Walker knew the joy of grandchildren. Their daughter, Mary Catherine, married Cecile Ritchie on January 3, 1944. Mary Catherine and Cecile had two daughters, Barbara and Karen Lee, and a son, Timothy. Thanks to Warren Wilson, Walker and Alice's nephew, I was able to connect with the granddaughters, who live in Chula Vista,

California. I learned that both Mary Catherine and Cecile are still alive, though in failing health.

Alice's granddaughter Barbara wrote a memory of her: "Our Grandma holds a very special place in my heart. She was the most kind-hearted, giving person I've ever met. She never had a harsh word to say to or about anyone. It's so sad she had such a hard childhood, but it helped mold her into the wonderful woman that she was."[166] Even so, Alice had her demons. Barbara remembers that she endured electroshock treatments sometime during her later years.[167]

Warren Wilson, Alice's nephew, also shared an affectionate memory. He had visited Aunt Alice and Uncle Warren in Covington for a week one summer when he was ten or twelve years old, probably in the late 1940s. By that time Mary Catherine had married and moved away, so Warren had their full attention. It is one of his fondest childhood memories.

Alice and Walker were very kind to him and took him to some very interesting places. Walker took him to his workplace and to a courthouse, where they saw a trial taking place. The three of them went to Devou Park and a baseball game. He remembers ice cream and taking a bath every day, whether he needed it or not. Warren didn't want to leave and go back home to the hot work of tobacco farming. Alice and Walker took the time to entertain a small boy, to help him expand his horizons and discover the pleasures of life in a city.

Alice died on September 8, 1971, at the age of seventy-one. She led a full life, perhaps the most balanced of any of the surviving children of Nick and Viola.

Rosa (sometimes spelled Rose), Nick and Viola's third child, remains the most enigmatic. She was born on September 10, either in 1902 or 1904. Family genealogy shows her birth date as 1902, but the 1910 census reports her as six years old, which means she was born in 1904. Her younger brother, Ray, was born in April 1905. If Rosa was born in 1904, Ray was born prematurely at seven months, and Viola would have had to become pregnant immediately after Rosa's birth. Later circuit court records signed by her guardian indicate that Rosa was "an infant over 14 years of age" in May 1917.[168] It's likely that Rosa was born in 1902.

If so, Rosa was about eight and a half years old at the time of her mother's death in 1911. Court records show that William E. Morgan of Highland County, Ohio, became Rosa's legal guardian. William Morgan's wife was Sarah Ragland, the daughter of John Ragland, who was probably related to the Judy family through Elizabeth Ragland, the first wife of Viola's father, James. Sarah and William Morgan were childless, and they may have been eager to bring Rosa into their household. According to my mother in *History of the Muntz Family*, "Rose Frances

Muntz was taken to raise by Will Morgan and his wife. There was little kinship. Will lived in Ohio and was a wealthy man."[169] On the surface Rose was a very fortunate girl; she would become the only child in a wealthy family.

In the 1920 federal census, Rosa appears in the Morgan household, as Rosa F. Morgan, age sixteen.[170] Unfortunately Rosa's new nuclear family was short-lived; Sarah died on August 24, 1926. Sometime between 1920 and 1930, Rosa married Wilbur M. Cheney, and the new couple continued to live in the William Morgan household.[171]

Wilbur Cheney, two years younger than Rosa, was born on January 11, 1904. Wilbur may have met Rosa through another family in the Morgan's neighborhood. Wilbur's mother's maiden name was Sallie Roush, and several Roush families appear on the same census page as the Morgan family. William Morgan died on September 18, 1930, presumably leaving his estate to Rosa. Mother's *History* makes only one succinct comment on the marriage of Rosa and Wilbur: "Rose married a man by the name of Chaney [*sic*] and he ran through her inheritance." [172]

No record exists of children from the marriage of Rosa and Wilbur. In the years between 1930 and1942, Rosa's mental health deteriorated to the point that, on January 1, 1940, she was committed to Athens State Hospital in Athens, Ohio. Rosa died there on August 17, 1942, not long before her fortieth birthday.

On her death certificate, Rosa's occupation is listed as "unemployed housewife" and her residence is listed as Lynchburg, Ohio. The principal cause of her death is "Pulmonary tuberculosis." The contributory cause listed is "Dementia Praecox."[173] At the time of her commitment, medical experts diagnosed dementia praecox as "precocious madness…a chronic, deteriorating psychotic disorder characterized by rapid cognitive disintegration."[174] The condition has since been relabeled as schizophrenia.

Wilbur survived Rosa and died on January 31, 1967. They are buried together in Barnes Cemetery in Fairview, Ohio.

Ray Edward Muntz, my grandfather, the fourth child of Nick and Viola, was born on April 12, 1905. He lived his whole life in Harrison County, Kentucky. Young Ray was probably already living in a different family household at the time of Viola's death in 1911. The 1910 federal census showed five-year-old Ray in Viola's household, but it also showed a five-year-old nephew named "Roy" living in the household of Ray's uncle, Walter Frank Muntz.[175]

Uncle Frank, Nick's younger brother, became Ray's guardian after Viola's death.[176] At the time of Nick's death, Frank was thirty years old and married. He and his wife, Bettie, had no other children, according to federal census records. Frank obviously regarded young Ray as his son, because when Frank died, he left him at least two pieces of rental property.[177] Surprisingly, Ray appeared in their household only in the 1910 census. In the 1920 census, when he was only fifteen years old, he is not listed.

Ray resurfaced at the age of nineteen, when he married my grandmother, Annie Alleene Sims Wilson, on May 24, 1924. Alleene was a young widow with a six-year-old son, Willie. Ray and Alleene had two children together: Charles Edward Muntz (my father), born on August 22, 1925, and Ray Edward Muntz Jr., born on July 27, 1930.

PHOTO OF RAY EDWARD MUNTZ WITH CHILDREN

The photo of Ray Edward Muntz with children was probably taken around 1932. Proud Ray has his

arms around his toddler son, Ray Jr. To his left is my father, Charles, who is about seven years old. The child in the back holding a puppy is Willie Wilson, Alleene's son by her first marriage.

My grandfather Ray spent most of his life on the railroad. He worked for the L&N Railroad as a section hand, and my dad remembered growing up in a series of railroad houses up and down the line:

> I lived in a lot of towns up and down the L&N Railroad because my dad worked on the railroad. And ever so often, him being the lowest man in seniority on that section, he would get what they called kicked off, and he would have to go to the next station, and kick in where they had seniority. And we lived all up and down from Poindexter to Berry, [to] Cynthiana…and I went to school as much as three different schools in one school year.[178]

Dad also remembered that his father was sent to the Cincinnati area, to the DeCoursey Railroad Yard in Kentucky during the Ohio River Great Flood of 1937. He and the other employees lived in railroad cars and helped rescue flood victims in boats. The life of a lineman was hard, and so was life for his family, but at least he had a job in the 1930s, when many did not.

In the 1950s "Pa" Muntz was a constant background in my life, a stocky, barrel-chested man in coveralls with a full head of nearly black hair. In my earliest memories, he was an immensely strong, laughing man who bounced me on his knees. Ray favored his father, Nick, in appearance. In the previously mentioned Muntz family picture, Nick's image is touchingly reminiscent of the Pa Muntz I knew as a little girl: a short man, about five-foot-eight, with a barrel chest. Pa's hair was also black and thick, a trademark of the Muntz family. His face was almost a baby face.

The summer I was eight or nine, my grandmother was in the hospital suffering from blood clots. Our family moved into town from the country to stay with my grandfather. The railroad house on North Walnut Street backed right up to the tracks, and the massive coal trains served as roaring clocks for us, barreling through several times a day. Mom cooked and cared for us all. She and Pa Muntz had a friendly, easy relationship, even though he was growing progressively deafer during these years.

He was also growing progressively distant. I remember him standing for hours, looking out at the same horizon, or sitting in a chair, staring at the floor, sighing occasionally. His solid German face was carved with the lines of a perpetual scowl. Only his dreams allowed his emotions a vent, for I would wake up in the night and hear his groans and outcries.

Sometime in my early teens, the family took him to a doctor who determined he was suffering from depression and needed electroshock treatments. Over the next several years, he endured numerous treatments yet continued to work. I remember him as totally withdrawn during that time, a silent presence when we stopped in after church on Sundays to spend the afternoon. Later I learned from Mom that part of Pa's problem was his boss on the railroad. For some reason his line boss held a grudge against him and rode him mercilessly on the job. He dealt with that year after year, probably because he saw no alternative. Mercifully, he became too deaf to work on the line, received a small pension, and retired.

It was then, in my high school and college years, that Pa became a presence in my life again. He began to laugh and take joy in our company. He started going to church with us, along with Ma Muntz, and suddenly the Muntz family took up almost a whole pew in the back of the church. One of his proudest moments came when the Cynthiana Baptist Church invited him to become an usher. For eight years he arrived punctually every Sunday morning and handed out bulletins at the sanctuary entrance, even though it was doubtful he ever heard a word of the sermon.

My older brother, Charlie, has a unique memory of Pa during Charlie's teenage years, when the two of them worked as part-time laborers at the Kentucky Cardinal Dairy, where my dad was a cheese maker:

> I worked at the dairy with Pa Muntz. He would get hired on to help load train cars, tractor trailers, with cheese…I was very adept at this task. So it was my job to teach him, help him, move those boxes of cheese around in tight spaces. He was

a very strong man, but fine muscles and flexibility were required. I think this is as close as I ever got to him. We developed a respect for each other that I cherish. He was a simple man, but at the same time I think he understood and perceived things far beyond what we ever knew. I think Ray Muntz lived out the tragedy of Nick…By God, he was a man.[179]

MUNTZ FAMILY SETTING TOBACCO

The photo of the Muntz family setting tobacco was taken in the 1960s. Seated on the back of the tractor, sorting tobacco sets, are my father Charles and grandfather Ray. Young brother Danny is standing. Except for the age of Danny, this scene could have occurred anytime over several decades.

In September of 1972, when I was married and living in northern Virginia, Pa Muntz suffered a stroke while helping Dad harvest his tobacco. We traveled back home to see him and found a limp, misshapen man in the hospital bed. The change in his appearance stunned me so much I recorded it in my journal.

> He was lying limply in bed and his eyes rolled a little when he saw us. He looked thin, and gaunter in the face, than usual. The deep tan was still there, but there was a tiredness, a frustration, that showed through. One side of his face drooped—it is the only way I know to describe it, and he leaned into his paralyzed side. When he recognized us and tried to speak, his voice sounded confused, drunken, a hard-fought-for slur. "I—I—I'm goin tuh die."
>
> I kissed him and shouted cheerfully into his ear, "Nonsense!" For years we had only communicated with him by shouting. And that always seemed acceptable to him, even preferable. I know there are times when he gleefully turned my grandmother off. But now he strained, almost desperately, to hear our words. His eyes glued to our lips, and he would watch with total concentration to understand,

> but often could not. He hadn't tried in
> so long…The attempts to communicate
> became agonizing, and after twenty min-
> utes we were grateful for the opportunity
> to flee. As I leaned over to kiss him good-
> bye, he gave me a heart-rending look of
> love mixed with despair. "I—I—I'm goin
> tuh die."[180]

Pa Muntz died Saturday, September 23, 1972, at
about 2:00 a.m. He was only sixty-seven years old.
The doctor was not sure what caused his death—
perhaps another heart attack, another stroke, a fluid
buildup in his lungs. He died alone, a fact I will
mourn for the rest of my life.

Ray Muntz probably knew one or two of his siblings. He is listed as a survivor at Charlie's funeral.
He almost certainly lost touch with Rose and Clara,
who moved out of state. Ray left behind two sons
and six grandchildren. Today his descendants
include eleven great-grandchildren and numerous
great-great-grandchildren, some of whom still bear
a resemblance to him.

James Kenneth Muntz, the fifth child of Viola
and Nick, was born on August 16, 1907. Kenneth
was only three years old when his mother died. In
court records Joseph Muntz is listed as Kenneth's
guardian, and a child aged twelve and identified

as a grandson, is listed in the 1920 federal census in Joseph's home. The child's name is recorded as "Junne," but a close look at the original record reveals it to be James. Apparently Joseph and his wife, Elizabeth, were still raising children when he was almost eighty years old.

Joseph Muntz died on April 7, 1920. Apparently Kenneth moved in with his uncle Roy after his grandfather's death. Kenneth is included in Roy's family photo with his brother Charlie. The youngest of the six people in the photo, he stands in the back to the right of his cousin, Doan Muntz, and just behind and to the left of Charlie. With his sober expression, necktie, and coat, the light-haired Kenneth seems to take his position seriously. Eloise Judy, in her 2008 interview, also remembered that Roy Muntz took in Kenneth. Perhaps he lived back and forth between the two families. Whatever the arrangement, Joseph Muntz and his descendants took care of their own.

As with most of the other children, few details exist about Kenneth's growing-up years. He first surfaces in public records with his marriage to Jessie Woodrow Florence in Harrison County on May 17, 1930.[181] This marriage was short-lived, and Kenneth remarried on January 21, 1933, this time to his lifelong wife, Virginia Langford. Kenneth and Virginia had ten children together, nine of whom survived. The names of the children, in order of birth, are Mary Alice Muntz Bolen, James Russell Muntz, Charles Ray Muntz, Della Frances Muntz, Margaret Muntz Lenora, Rose Sue Muntz Tyree, Mary Catherine Muntz (stillborn),

Carl Douglas Muntz, Joseph Edward Muntz, and Paul Kenneth Muntz.

The oldest child, Mary Alice Bolen, was born in 1935. She remembers living in Peewee Valley, Kentucky, and then moving to Mauckport, Indiana, where she grew up, but doesn't remember why the family made those moves. "My father was a share-cropper farmer. We had a house to live in and a garden. We had two mules and a wagon."[182] Like his brothers, Charlie and Ray, Kenneth lived by his hands, making a life for his family with hard physical toil.

Mary Alice also remembers that her father was involved in an accident, sometime in the 1950s, while cutting down a tree. She was about eighteen when it happened. The tree fell on him, causing a disabling head injury. He eventually went into a nursing home after her mother's death in 1967. That would mean Kenneth spent the last twenty-five years of his life in a nursing home. The Social Security Death Index shows that he died in March 1992 in Pekin, Indiana.[183] Kenneth's grandson Robert Muntz remembers that his grandfather resided in a nursing home in Salem, Indiana. Robert's Uncle Charlie and Aunt Evelyn, a nurse, lived in Pekin and managed Kenneth's affairs.[184] Apparently family members stayed in Kenneth's life and cared for him until the end.

Four of Kenneth and Virginia's children—James, Charles, Francis, and Susan—have since died. But the list of the descendants of Kenneth and Virginia is impressive: nine children, twenty-three grandchildren, and many more great-grandchildren.

———————————————

Clara, the youngest child of Viola and Nick Muntz, was born February 19, 1910. Eight days earlier, her father had committed suicide. Four days before her birth, her grandfather Joseph Muntz petitioned the Harrison County Court to become administrator of her father's estate, stating that Clara's mother Viola was so ill she "is feeble-minded."[185] Almost certainly Clara had little contact with her mother during the next year. Court records show that she was cared for by her Aunt Laura Muntz Whitaker. When Viola died in the Lexington Asylum on April 3, 1911, of "exhaustion following acute mania," Clara was just over a year old.[186]

Clara's Aunt Laura was thirty-nine years old in 1911. She had been married to Volney Whitaker for eighteen years, and their only child, Frances, was eighteen. Both Laura and Volney grew up in Harrison County, but by 1906 the family had moved to Shelbyville, Indiana, where they would live the rest of their lives. It is unclear why they left Kentucky. Volney was a carpenter, and perhaps work led him north.

Laura and Volney brought infant Clara into their household when their own daughter was practically grown. Although no written record exists, Laura probably rescued Clara soon after her birth and took her back to Indiana. Ed Judy was still listed as Clara's guardian in 1917 when the homestead was sold and divided among the six orphans. The only record that shows Laura's involvement with Clara is the 1913 final settlement of Viola Judy's estate. In the list of monies distributed to Viola's children, the amount of ten dollars is recorded as having already been paid to Laura Whitaker on Clara's behalf.

VOLNEY WHITAKER FAMILY

Clara was a member of the Volney Whitaker household in the 1920 census, listed as a nine-year-old niece. Daughter Frances is living in the same household, married to Albert Brunner. An undated photograph shows the whole family standing on a sidewalk dressed as if for church. It is summertime;

the tree behind them is full and shady; the men have removed their jackets and are dressed in shirts and ties. One of the men has his sleeves rolled up. Lined up, from left to right, are Volney and Laura Whitaker, Clara, an unidentified man, Frances Brunner, and Albert Brunner. Their young son, Donald Brunner, stands in front of his grandmother Laura, her hands draped around his shoulders. Donald appears to be five or six, so the photo was probably taken around 1925. (Albert Brunner, Donald's father, died two years later of "prolonged illness from carcinoma," so Laura and Volney continued to have a child growing up in their home for years.)[187]

Clara, in the center in a street-length dress with a ruffled hem, is easily the most striking figure in the photograph. The tallest person in the group, her hair is cut into a neat brunette bob that frames her face. Although she is not smiling, her features are attractive. She appears to be well cared for, nestled in the center of this family portrait. She is probably about fifteen years old.

In the 1930 federal census, Clara is no longer in the Volney Whitaker household. She appears as a roomer in the home of William and Ethyl Hecht in Cincinnati, Ohio.[188] Her occupation is listed as private duty nurse. Clara graduated from Bethesda School of Nursing sometime before that. Her obituary states that Clara "was employed at Major Hospital in Cincinnati…in the 1940s," but it was probably during the 1930s.[189] Obviously she was an intelligent and independent young woman.

By the time of Laura Whitaker's death in 1938, Clara was married to Herbert Zike and living in Morristown, Indiana.[190] Clara and Herbert had a daughter, Judith Ann, born on December 7, 1946. Her life appears to be fulfilled, both in family and career.

Here, however, the happy ending unravels. By 1956 Clara was a patient at Madison State Hospital in Madison, Indiana, a sprawling mental institution along the banks of the Ohio River. She never left Madison. When she died on January 1, 1975, she had been a patient there for over eighteen years. What had happened to cause her mental illness?

A resourceful librarian in the Shelby County [Indiana] Public Library helped locate Judith Ann Zike, Clara's daughter. Judith, like her mother, studied nursing, and she graduated from Ball State University. She married Timothy Gabbard in 1969; they had two children over the years and moved to California and later to Florida. Today Judith is a hospice nurse and has been for twenty-two years.

Speaking with Judith on the phone, I was surprised by how much we have in common. She and I were born nine days apart; we both have two children and four grandchildren. But due to the idiosyncrasy of birth generations, her mother was my great aunt. Sadly, she had little to contribute about Clara's illness. Judith has only vague memories of Clara because she was just ten years old when her mother was committed to Madison State Hospital. She remembers her mom's anger but could not share any specific memories. Judith said that when she was a little girl, a lady who lived upstairs in her house helped care for her.[191]

Judith also revealed that Herbert, her father, was blind from the age of nineteen or twenty. Born in 1909, he was fifteen months younger than Clara, so he would have been blind in 1930, when Clara started a career in nursing. Perhaps their affection for one another began because she was caring for him. Herbert later divorced Clara and was remarried to Martha Bender. According to his obituary, he died on August 15, 1986, after a long career as a milk distributor.[192]

In spite of all the pluses in her life—a caring adopting family, education, and a husband and daughter of her own—Clara lost her way and, like two of her siblings, Charlie and Rosa, died in a mental institution.

Most of the descendants of Nick and Viola lived lives that ended in suffering and caused suffering for their families. Perhaps the legacy of the tragedy of Nick and Viola lay over them like a pall that could not be thrown off in one generation. Perhaps they inherited genetic characteristics that caused these mental conditions and robbed them of predictable lives. Two of Viola's brothers, Virgil and James, committed suicide late in life. A cloud of sadness hangs over both the Judys and the Muntzes in these two generations.

Of course the story doesn't end with the lives and deaths of Viola and Nick's children. Many children, grandchildren, and great-grandchildren are living out the story today. Until recently most of them did not know about their Kentucky ancestors, who brought six children into the world with the hope of a prosperous future but instead lost everything. Perhaps this story can be read as a reflection on the blessings we all enjoy in our world today, where enormous strides have been made in medical diagnosis and treatment; where society does not condemn those who suffer mental illness; where there are safety nets for families in hard times; where king tobacco has been slain, at least in the economy of the rural South.

In the 1980s my mother began this research into my father's family past. She sent me a letter about the portrait she discovered of the Joseph Muntz family (featured on page four), taken near the end of the nineteenth century:

> After working on this history, you get the weirdest feeling that you really know them all. It was nice to know that all of Pa Muntz's brothers and sisters were taken in by people in that picture with the exception of Rose, after the death of their parents. Look closely at the Laura in the picture. I feel like I can see you in her… Any little bit of information that you find,

I guess, tends to personalize the people in
the picture.[193]

Toward the end of my research and writing of
this book, I felt the same way as my mother. I have
even allowed myself to fantasize about a Muntz
family reunion—not a reunion of those of us living
today, but of all those whose lives were so dramati-
cally changed by the tobacco wars in the early twentieth century in Kentucky.

Everyone is gathered back at the Joseph Muntz
homestead off Salem Pike. It is summertime; the
trees are full of leaves, and shirtsleeves are rolled up.
Joseph and Elizabeth, proud grandparents, preside
over all the children and grandchildren gathered
there. A feast will be served up from chickens killed
and dressed this morning, corn shucked right out of
the field, half-runner green beans cooked with a little
pork belly, and fresh tomatoes. Blackberry cobbler
and homemade ice cream will create a perfect coda
to the day. Around the table set out in the yard are
lots of cousins, but the ones my eyes are drawn to are
the children of Nick and Viola, who sit side by side,
laughing and bouncing baby Clara. Sweet Alice is
helping set the table, while an irrepressible Rosa
races after Charlie and Ray and Kenneth in some
version of tag. The burley crop is coming along fine,
blessed with rains at the right time and no late frost.
Corn and hay are plentiful, and quarts and quarts
of beans, corn, cucumber pickles, and blackberries
grace the shelves of the cellar. In the hills behind the

house, puffy cumulus clouds boil up in the sky. But for a moment—the dance of life and death stops, and peace reigns. For a moment—the kingdom of heaven is present in the midst of them all.

Reflections

In 1946, the year I was born, the culture of tobacco still thrived. As it had for Nick and Viola, it determined the lives of my parents growing up in the 1920s and 1930s, it surrounded our family in the 1950s and 1960s, and it would continue to be an economic and social force through the end of the century. Today, knowing the devastating impact of tobacco on health, I am almost embarrassed by the pride we felt in our tobacco crop.

In the early springs, as we drove back and forth to and from Cynthiana in Daddy's truck, farmers all around us burned their tobacco beds and covered the tiny seeds with white muslin. The burning fires and smoke curling up into the sky seemed inviting as we drove by. In the summers we played in the empty tobacco barn, climbing the rails against our parents' warnings. Tobacco sticks became horses with baling twine reins that we cowboys and Indians galloped around on. My earliest summer memories include fields of tobacco on both sides of the road as far as the eye could see, growing gigantic as the summer progressed. In fall, on Highway 27 that ran beside our front yard, we counted the heavily loaded tobacco wagons, pulled by trucks and tractors, heading for the auction warehouse.

And of course, the members of our family were faithful consumers of the product we raised. My grandfather Ray loved a good chew, as much as my grandmother Alleene despised its juice. Unlike my parents, who smoked unfiltered Camels most of their lives, Pa kept his pouch of Bull Durham inside his coveralls and pulled it out discreetly for a comforting chew now and then. Both my brothers smoked; my sister smoked. For some reason I did not, but I craved the fragrance of secondhand tobacco smoke. My mother smoked until the day she died at the age of eighty-two. As she used to say, "Everybody is allowed one vice." It was her only one.

One of the things I appreciate today is the stationary quality of our world. The same names reappeared decade after decade: LeBus, Swinford, Smiser, Judy, Muntz. Families stayed in the same county for generations, and often sons stepped into the careers of their fathers.

The LeBus family was an economic force in Nick's time, in my grandfathers' time, and in my father's time. In the 1930s in Harrison County, when my father helped house his grandfather Simms's tobacco crops, he was housing LeBus tobacco. After my father came home from World War II, he used the GI Bill to go to school to become a cheese maker. The cheese plant where he went to work, the Kentucky Cardinal Dairy on Highway 27, just across the bridge from downtown Cynthiana, was owned by Jim Whitt, whose wife was a LeBus. The LeBus family would write my dad's paycheck for the next twenty-four years, until the plant closed in 1970.

The Swinford family name conjures up lawyers and judges. Judge Mac Swinford was an institution when I was growing up in Harrison County. He was the son of M.C. Swinford, the lawyer who defended Nick Muntz in 1909. Mac Swinford also served as a federal judge and wrote the nation's first desegregation order in 1955. Mac's daughter, Sally, was my high school English teacher in the 1960s.

My maternal great-grandfather, Tom Simms, kept hound dogs for Judge Mac Swinford. Mac and other prominent landowners loved to go foxhunting, and Tom kept a fox penned up for those events. One childhood summer my dad found the fox in an empty silo and killed it, thinking he was doing a good deed. Grandpa Simms was not happy when young Charlie proudly presented the carcass.

The name "Smiser" equals "doctor" in Harrison County, even in my generation. When I was growing up, our family doctor was Tod Smiser, the son of Dr. J.W. Smiser who performed Elva Coy's inquest in 1910. Tod Smiser had an acerbic personality but loved his patients. He saved my mother's life when her fourth child, Sharon, was stillborn in 1954. My mother loved Dr. Smiser as well. When her fifth child, Danny, was born several years later, she named him Danny Tod Muntz. I doubt that Tod Smiser knew the connection between his father and my great-grandfather Nick. If he had, he would have found something ironic to say about it.

But the ritual of raising tobacco was the real constant in the life of Harrison County for genera-

tions. In his later years, my dad recollected his childhood days in the 1930s, when he spent his summers
with Grandpa Simms. He remembered helping set
tobacco using a plow called the Rastus plow. "Usually the walking plow was one horse, and what they
called a Rastus plow was a plow that had three shov-
els on it, and you'd run twic't in a row. You'd run
onc't on this side and then you'd come back and onc't
on that side, and that kindly furrowed your soil up
around your crop."[194] My dad fondly remembered
a notorious horse named John Dillinger, owned by
the LeBus family. The obstinate horse was "a good
workhorse, but you couldn't get up on him."[195] Perhaps my great-grandfather Nick, who had a team of
horses, had a Rastus cultivator.

Mom also grew up on a tenant tobacco farm, one
of six girls in the family of Calvert and Nellie Shaw,
struggling to survive in Bourbon County during the
Depression. Hearing her memories, I realized that
life had not changed much in those three decades
between Viola's death and Mom's childhood. "Daddy
was unfortunate not to have any sons…so we had to
pull our weight…we helped with the chopping of the
weeds. We would follow the setter to see that the plants
all got into the ground. [We] never done a whole lot in
the housing end of it, hand off the wagon maybe."[196]

Like Viola, my maternal grandmother, Nellie,
cooked without electricity. "She cooked…on a coal
stove, and she had these iron skillets, and she would
fill those skillets full of lard. She would brown her
chicken…and then she would push it to the back

of the stove, and it would sit there and simmer for hours."[197] But chicken was a "Sunday preacher coming to dinner" dish. Most of the time, the family ate whatever came out of the garden or what they had canned. Tobacco money clothed them and helped them buy the necessities they couldn't grow.

Like Nick and Viola, my mom and dad watched the skies for rain, but they prayed the thunderstorms would not bring hail. My dad only raised about three-tenths of an acre of tobacco, but he and Mom watched the weather anxiously all through the growing season. She even kept a daily diary of the weather, worrying when they needed rain and rejoicing when it came.

And when the crop was housed, Mom and Dad spent many hours in the stripping room in the fall and early winter. The loose-leaf process was long and tedious, but my dad, just like Nick, took pride in the symmetrical layout of his baskets.

Of course, not everything was the same as in Nick and Viola's time. When I was growing up, we had tractors and mechanical setters to help get the crop in the ground. Dad used chemical sprays, both for worms and suckers, whereas in Nick's day the only way to control the worms was to walk the rows and pick them off by hand and kill them. The chemicals used in the 1950s were highly toxic. I remember Dad coming in from the field one hot summer day and lying down on the couch. He was nauseous and did not move for a long time, sickened by the chemicals he had sprayed.

Fortunately for my parents' generation, the federal government controlled the base price for tobacco, setting a minimum that each farmer would be paid. No matter how dry the year or unsatisfactory the crop, a farmer who raised tobacco was assured of a base income. To control supply and demand, the government also instituted a limitation on acreage and designated which farms would receive a tobacco allotment. To enforce the acreage limits, employees of the ASCS (Agricultural Stabilization and Conservation Service) actually measured and destroyed tobacco that extended beyond the farms' allotments.

During my college years, from 1964 to 1966, I was a summer employee for this rather messy control program. A job at the ASCS office was the best summer job a teenager could land in Harrison County. College boys were hired to go out into the fields and measure a farmer's plot of tobacco. They brought the measurements back into the office, where college girls, serving as seasonal office staff, calculated the area of the measured acreage and determined whether a farmer had produced over his allotment. If the figures showed he had, then the boys were sent back to the fields to destroy the extra acreage, literally hacking it down with knives and scythes. For obvious reasons, our calculations did not always make the office popular with individual farmers. We had to check our figures over and over, and the boys were often sent out to re-measure. But we had a good time in the office and ate lunch out at Renaker's Drug Store and the Dairy Queen. It never burdened us girls, who were endowed with a high sense of our own significance, that our work seriously affected farmers' lives and incomes.

All that tobacco raised in the 1950s and 1960s ended up at the tobacco warehouses in downtown Cynthiana near the railroad tracks. Most of those massive structures are still standing today, symbols of wealth and authority, albeit empty symbols since the collapse of the tobacco market in the last twenty years. But even as late as the 1980s, the power and magic were still present when farmers hauled their crops in to be sold.

In 1984 my family traveled from our home in Iowa back to Kentucky for Thanksgiving. Dad invited us to join him for a visit to the LeBus warehouse on the opening day of tobacco sales.

Growing up, I had never been inside the tobacco houses that sprawl on the edge of downtown, covering acres of real estate. I remember their awesome size through the eyes of a child. One of them, LeBus Warehouse Number Two, is a venerable red brick building, occupying a city block downtown on Church Street, winged by two other cavernous warehouses named for the families who built them: Pepper, Peak and Florence, and Wiglesworth & Sons. Another LeBus warehouse was razed in 2001. When I was growing up, the area of downtown Cynthiana along the railroad tracks was dominated by these massive structures, and others that are gone now. The McLoney warehouse burned to the ground in a spectacular fire on a summer Sunday morning in

1960 while I was sitting in church a few blocks away, mesmerized by the sounds of fire sirens screaming continuously through the beleaguered pastor's sermon.

The warehouse we visited in the 1980s, though, was not downtown. It was a new edifice out on Republican Pike, built out of metal that looked like corrugated tin. We walked into a front area with an office and waiting room, where checks were cut for farmers who had sold their crop. Beyond this anteroom loomed the charged space of the tobacco-filled warehouse, alive with sellers and buyers and even a camera crew from a Lexington TV station. Dad prided himself on having his tobacco stripped, and on the floor, the first day government graders and tobacco company buyers walked the aisles. And that was this day, the Friday after Thanksgiving.

When we walked into the warehouse, the heavy spice of the massed tobacco bombarded our senses. The rich and tantalizing aroma literally made the air denser. Half the warehouse was stacked with long rows of bales; the other half was empty. Dad explained that this custom kept the buyers moving from one warehouse to another. The bales were three by four feet, the height of my chest and the size of a large shipping crate. They varied in size depending on the type of leaf in the bale: flyings, lugs, or red. That year, my dad said, the buyers were supposedly valuing darker, redder leaf.

"Why?" I asked. "Is it better?"

"It's just what they want."[198]

On a few of the palettes were baskets of hand-stripped and tied tobacco, leaves of a like color bunched into a hand, then tied together with another leaf and laid on the circular baskets with the ties radiating out from the center. A few years earlier, every palette would have been covered with these symmetrical laboriously hand-tied leaves, representing thousands of long, cold hours in the stripping room. A revolution had recently occurred with the introduction of baler boxes, where leaves of like kind were laid and pressed down to a certain bulk and then tied with twine. The younger farmers tried it first, and the older ones resisted it. The fact that my dad had built his first baler boxes this year was a sign that the trend was here to stay.

Even though he did not depend on his tobacco crop for a living, Dad had an emotional investment in the price his crop brought. The government graders appeared and moved swiftly down the aisles, fingering a leaf here, ruffling a bale there, and then marking a card and laying it on top. Dad was right behind them as they graded. I watched the profile of his face, his eyes locked on their hands, his mouth working strangely, set in lockjaw with a twitch around his lips. His tension was so sudden and complete it infected me too.

When the graders passed on, he came behind them, lifted the cards with his back to us, and then turned with a look of glee in his eyes. "They gave me eight cents better than I expected on the lugs, four cents better on the flyings…that should average out to about a dollar eighty-nine for the crop per pound." He was at ease now, joking to Mom, "Hedy, we can go out to lunch after all."

Unlike the warehouses, many of the landmarks of the past are gone now or changed beyond recognition. Nearly a century after great-grandfather Nick's suicide, my brother Charlie and I walked the farm where Viola and Nick had lived. It was a perfect crisp October day, sunny and about sixty-five degrees. The trees and sumac were ripening red on the ridges and in the hollows. We were guided to the site of the Judy homestead and barn by Charline and Warren Wilson, neighbors who own much of the bordering land. None of the land around here is farmed much anymore but is set aside for hunting.

The rough rutted lane down to the site of the homestead is still named, aptly enough, Hazard Lane. From the cattle gate, we walked through a peaceful landscape. The sky was pure blue, the sun sparkled on the grass, and a gentle breeze caressed our hair. Suddenly I felt a shiver, and at the same moment Charlie asked, "Is this the lane where Nick shot Elva Coy?" It was, Charline and Warren confirmed. "At about this spot, probably."

Not far from there, the lane ended at a level area grown up in thistles and dry grasses. Some signs of a former dwelling, concrete blocks and glass, revealed the home site. According to Charline, the house was still standing into the 1980s, when it burned. From her memory, the original Judy homestead was a large house. It was hard even to see the footprint now through the tall grasses blown by the breeze. A little farther on, behind the house, stood a barn, but not the barn Nick walked to in 1910. It too had burned, but this barn was built on the same site. Just off to the left was the Judy family cemetery. We found several stones facedown, some broken. No names were discernible—only one date, 1884. Charline was distressed at the condition of the cemetery, how it had deteriorated since the last time she had been out there. Standing together, on the edge of the old family cemetery, we felt the sacred quality of the space. Silently we walked back to the truck.

Wandering through another graveyard in 2007, my brother Charlie came upon Elva Coy's gravesite and headstone. The headstone memorializes David Coy, Elva's father, and Elva, buried side by side. It is a plain limestone square with a simple stone heart carved in the top. That summer a small clump of white plastic flowers adorned the grave. Someone still honors the Coy family. Do they know the story behind Elva's death?

When my mother began genealogy research in 1980, she unlocked the mystery of the Muntz family. She unearthed photographs, found old graveyards, located newspaper articles, and pieced together the outline of my father's past. She wrote to me about her discoveries and how much they meant to my dad and uncle. But I was a busy young woman then— wife, mother, professional—who didn't have time for such things.

Now my mother and father are gone. My grandfather Ray, all his siblings, and Nick and Viola are gone. Life seems to be not so much about what I have accomplished as it is about what I have received, what I owe to those who came before me. I can never pay them back—only pay forward by sharing their story.

Notes

Introduction

1 T.H. Breen, *Tobacco Culture: The Mentality of the Great Tidewater Planters on the Eve of Revolution* (Princeton, 1987), 203.

2 Tracy Campbell, *The Politics of Despair* (Lexington, KY: 1993), 26–29.

Chapter 1

3 William Henry Perrin, ed., *History of Bourbon, Scott, Harrison and Nicholas Counties of Kentucky* (Chicago: O.L. Baskin & Co., 1882), 692.

4 Gum blankets, or rubberized canvas blankets, were common issue in the Civil War. If overheated, the gum resin melted.

5 *History of Bourbon.*

6 U.S. Census Bureau, Tenth Census, 1880, and Thirteenth Census, 1910, Buena Vista, Harrison, Kentucky, s.v. "Joseph Muntz," Ancestry.com. http://www.ancestry.com (accessed 2006).

7 Harrison County Court, "Harrison County Deeds and County Clerk Records," Deed Book 56 (Cynthiana, KY: 1894), 256.

8 Ibid., Deed Book 75, 411.

9 Campbell, *Politics*, 18–19.

10 W.F. Axton, *Tobacco and Kentucky* (Lexington, KY: University of Kentucky Press, 1975), 76.

11 Campbell, *Politics*, 19.

Chapter 2

12 R.B. Davis, "Tobacco Culture," *Eastern Reflector* (Greenville, NC: East Carolina University), February 19, 1890.

13 Ibid.

14 *Encyclopaedia Britannica*, 1911, s.v. "Tobacco," www.1911encyclopediabritannica.org/ Tobacco (accessed October 21, 2006).

Chapter 3

15 Axton, *Tobacco*, 87.

16 Campbell, *Politics*, 22.

17 Ibid., 23.

18 Axton, *Tobacco*, 83.

19 Campbell, *Politics*, 23.

20 Ibid., 24.

21 Ibid., 150.

22 "17 Cents for Tobacco," *The Log Cabin*, December 14, 1906. Two weekly newspapers existed in Harrison County during this period: *The Log Cabin* and *The Cynthiana Democrat*. Most of my references come from *The Log Cabin* because microfilm was

not available for the *Democrat* for the years 1906–1908 at the time of my research. Some 1909 references are from *The Cynthiana Democrat.*

23 Black patch tobacco was so named because the tobacco leaf was dark. It was grown primarily in the area where the Planters Protective Association was formed. A different type of tobacco, white burley, was grown in the Bluegrass Region of Kentucky.

24 Campbell, *Politics,* 76–77.

25 "To the Burley Grower," May 18, 1906; "Burley Growers Co.," July 6, 1906; "Tobacco Organization," October 19, 1906; "Tobacco Organization!" November 9, 1906; *Log Cabin.*

26 "The New Pledge," Ibid., December 7, 1906.

27 Ibid.

28 "Tobacco Men," Ibid., December 14, 1906.

29 *Lexington Leader,* December 8, 1907, quoted in Campbell, 135.

30 "Tobacco Men," *Log Cabin,* December 14, 1906.

31 In some accounts, Sylvan Dell is spelled Sylvandell or Sylvandale.

32 "Tobacco Growers," *Log Cabin,* December 14, 1906.

33 "Tobacco Sales," Ibid., December 7, 1906.

34 "17 Cts. For Tobacco," Ibid., December 14, 1906.

35 John van Willigan and Susan C. Eastwood, *Tobacco Culture: Farming Kentucky's Burley Belt* (Lexington, KY: The University Press of Kentucky, 1998), 143.

36 Axton, *Tobacco*, 30.

37 "Tobacco Sales," December 7, 1906; "521 Hogsheads," March 27, 1908, *Log Cabin*.

38 van Willigan and Eastwood, *Tobacco Culture*, 146.

39 Ibid., 150.

Chapter 4

40 "Tobacco Society Secures 59 Per Cent of Crop and the Pool Formed," *Log Cabin*, January 4, 1907.

41 "Tobacco Plans," Ibid., January 25, 1907.

42 "Tobacco Growers," Ibid., February 1, 1907.

43 "Tobacco News," Ibid., March 22, 1907.

44 "Show Your Colors," Ibid., April 19, 1907.

45 "Big Burley Barbecue," Ibid., April 26, 1907.

46 van Willigen and Eastwood, *Tobacco Culture*, 108.

Chapter 5

47 "Death of Clarence LeBus Ends Remarkable Business Career," *Log Cabin*, June 22, 1928.

48 Ibid.

49 "Death is a Distinct Loss," *The Cynthiana Democrat*, June 21, 1928.

50 Campbell, *Politics*, 108.

51 Ibid., 109.

52 "Tobacco Society," *Log Cabin*, January 4, 1907.

53 "Tobacco Growers," Ibid., February 1, 1907.

54 "Pooled Tobacco All Sold!" Ibid., November 20, 1908.

55 "Mr. Lebus Given Credit," Ibid., December 4, 1908.

56 "Tobacco Trust Loses!" Ibid., November 18, 1908.

57 Ibid., April 3, 1908.

58 Campbell, *Politics*, 129.

59 "Protest about Tobacco Money Deposits," *Cynthiana Democrat*, January 7, 1909.

60 Ibid., June 10, 1909.

61 "War is Over," Ibid., August 12, 1909.

62 "The Burley Society Contract," Ibid., September 2, 1909.

63 "Tobacco Meeting," Ibid., September 9, 1909.

64 Ibid., September 23, 1909.

65 "Tobacco Meeting," *Log Cabin*, July 1, 1910.

66 Ibid.

67 Ibid., September 16, 1910.

68 "Burley Society," *Log Cabin*, July 15, 1910.

69 "1910 Burley Pool Declared Off!" Ibid., October 21, 1910.

70 Campbell, *Politics*, 152.

71 Axton, *Tobacco*, 121.

72 van Willigen and Eastwood, *Tobacco Culture*, 55–58.

73 *Log Cabin*, June 22, 1928.

Chapter 6

74 *Log Cabin*, October 4, 1907.

75 Ibid., November 29, 1907.

76 Ibid., November 15, 1907.

77 Ibid., February 21, 1908.

78 "Leesburg," *Cynthiana Democrat*, February 25, 1909.

79 *Log Cabin*, May 15, 1908.

80 Ibid., March 20, 1908.

81 "Millersburg College Burned," Ibid., October 11, 1907.

82 John E. Kleber, ed., *The Kentucky Encyclopedia*, Third Printing (Lexington, KY: University Press of Kentucky, 1992), 638.

83 *History of Bourbon*, 312.

84 Commonwealth of Kentucky, Harrison County School District Records, Census

Report of District No. 3, State of Kentucky, County of Harrison: For School Year Ending June 30 1896 and 1897, Cynthiana, Kentucky.

85 Jeffrey Duvall, "Knowing about the Tobacco: Women, Burley, and Farming in the Central Ohio River Valley," *The Register of the Kentucky Historical Society 108*, no. 4 (Autumn 2010), 317.

86 David P. Searles, *A College for Appalachia: Alice Lloyd on Caney Creek* (Lexington, KY: The University Press of Kentucky, 1995), 33 and 47.

87 "The Burley Tobacco Society Contract," *Cynthiana Democrat*, September 2, 1909.

88 "Tobacco Supplement to the Cynthiana Democrat," Ibid.

89 "Big Day for Burley," Ibid., July 29, 1909.

90 "Cassius M. Clay Answers Miss Lloyd's Reply," Ibid., September 9, 1909.

91 "No Government Suit," Ibid., January 28, 1910.

Chapter 7

92 Campbell, *Politics*, 83.

93 Ibid., 12.

94 "Tobacco Meeting," *Log Cabin*, November 15, 1907.

95 "Tobacco Scare," Ibid., December 13, 1907.

96 Ibid.

97 Ibid.

98 "Tobacco Conference," Ibid., December 20, 1907.

99 "Night Riders," Ibid., March 20, 1908.

100 Ibid., March 27, 1908.

101 Ibid.

102 "Farmer Shot to Death," Ibid., May 29, 1908.

103 "Kentucky Farmer Whipped," Ibid., July 24, 1908.

104 "Entire Family Paid Penalty," Ibid., October 9, 1908.

105 "American Citizen," Ibid., May 8, 1908.

Chapter 8

106 "Burned Out," *The Cynthiana Democrat*, December 9, 1909.

107 "Night Walkers" and "Peace Army," *Log Cabin*, January 10, 1908.

108 "Peace Army's Good Work," Ibid., January 17, 1908.

109 "Threatening Note," Ibid., January 31, 1908.

110 "Barn Burned," Ibid., February 28, 1908.

111 "Barn Burned in Bracken," Ibid., March 13, 1908.

112 "Night Riders," Ibid., March 20, 1908.

113 "Militia Withdrawn," Ibid., January 24, 1908.

114 "Raid by Night Riders," and "Soldiers," Ibid., April 24, 1908 and May 1, 1908.

115 "Not Guilty!" Ibid., June 19, 1908.

116 "Night Riders," Ibid., March 20, 1908.

117 "American Citizen," Ibid., May 8, 1908.

118 "Night Riders," Ibid., July 31, 1908.

119 Campbell, *Politics, 127.*

120 *Log Cabin*, November 6, 1908.

121 *The Kentucky Encyclopedia*, 682.

Chapter 9

122 "Shot Down," *Cynthiana Democrat*, December 16, 1909.

123 U.S. Census Bureau, Twelfth Census, 1900, s.v. "David Coy," Ancestry.com (accessed 2011).

124 *Cynthiana Democrat*, December 16, 1909.

125 Ibid.

126 Ibid.

127 Ibid.

Chapter 10

128 "Hanged Himself," *Cynthiana Democrat*, February 17, 1910.

129 Philip A. Naff, "M.C. Swinford," *Biographies of Harrison County, Kentucky*, www.HarrisonCountyKy.US, 31 (accessed February 9, 2012).

130 "Shot Down," *Cynthiana Democrat*, December 16, 1909.

131 Mac Swinford, *Kentucky Lawyer* (Lexington, KY: The University Press of Kentucky, 2008), 117–118.

132 *Cynthiana Democrat*, December 16, 1909.

133 Harrison County Court Examining Trial, "Subpoena," December 11, 1909," Kentucky Department of Libraries and Archives (KDLA), Frankfort, KY, Box 65.

134 Ibid., "Commonwealth of Kentucky vs. Nicholas Muntz, December 13, 1909."

135 *Cynthiana Democrat*, December 16, 1909.

136 Harrison County Court Examining Trial, "Affidavit, December 13, 1909."

137 Ibid., "Commonwealth vs. Muntz."

138 Ibid., "Bail Bond, December 13, 1909." The bail bond lists J.T. McCauley but the 1910 census does not list a J.T. McCauley. J. F. McCauley was a neighbor of Nick Muntz on Salem Road.

139 *Cynthiana Democrat*, February 17, 1910.

140 Ibid.

Chapter 11

141 *Cynthiana Democrat*, February 17, 1910.

142 Harrison County Court, "In the Matter of Granting Administration the Personal

Estate of Geo. N. Muntz Deceased," 1910, Order Book 4, 289.

143 Ibid., "G. N. Muntz Inventory and Appraisements," Inventory Book 7, 289.

144 Ibid.

145 U.S. Census Bureau, Thirteenth Census, 1910, s.v. "Viola Muntz."

146 Harrison County Court, "Final Settlement," Inventory Book 7, 439.

147 Commonwealth of Kentucky State Board of Health Bureau of Vital Statistics, "Certificate of Death," Frankfort, Kentucky,1911, #9199.

148 *Log Cabin*, April 7, 1911.

149 Harrison County Court, "Viola Muntz Inventory and Appraisement," Inventory Book 7, 468.

150 Ibid.

151 Ibid., 491.

152 Campbell, *Politics*, 152–153.

Chapter 12

153 Harrison County Court, "Viola Muntz Final Settlement," Inventory Book 8, 263.

154 Harrison Circuit Court, "On Petition," KDLA, June 19, 1916, Frankfort, Kentucky, Box 57, 39-41.

155 Ibid., "Deposition for Plaintiff," September 6, 1916.

156 Harrison County Court, "Will of A.J. Pope," Will Book M, 318, March 24, 1908.

157 Ibid., "Charles Muntz & C by Com.," Deed Book 81, 384–386.

158 U.S. Census Bureau, Fourteenth Census, 1920, Claysville, Harrison County, Kentucky s.v. "Charlie Muntz" (accessed June 10, 2010).

159 Eloise Judy (wife of Edgar Judy, son of Virgil and Laura Belle Judy), Interview by Charles E. Muntz, Jr., October 20, 2009.

160 Jane Muntz Kearns (daughter of Charlie Muntz), Interview with author, June 17, 2011.

161 Commonwealth of Kentucky State Board of Health Bureau of Vital Statistics, "Certificate of Death," 1947, #648.

162 Eloise Judy, 2009.

163 U.S. Census Bureau, Ninth Census, 1870, Buena Vista, Harrison, Kentucky, s.v. "Lou Ann Judy" (accessed April 22, 2011).

164 Ibid., Fourteenth Census, 1920, Cynthiana, Harrison, Kentucky, s.v. "Alice Muntz" (accessed September 15, 2011).

165 Karen Lee Ritchie Schimak (granddaughter of Alice Muntz Wilson), E-Mail Conversation with author, April 22, 2010.

166 Barbara Ritchie Paiva (granddaughter of Alice Muntz Wilson), E-Mail Conversation with author, May 11, 2010.

167 Barbara Ritchie Paiva, Telephone Conversation with author, December 2011.

168 Harrison Circuit Court, "On Petition."

169 Hedy Muntz, *History of the Muntz Family* (unpublished manuscript, August 19–21, 1988), iv.

170 Census, Fourteenth Census, 1920, Hamer, Highland, Ohio, s.v. "Wm. E. Morgan" (accessed June 12, 2010).

171 U.S. Census Bureau, Fifteenth Census, 1930, s.v. "William E. Morgan" (accessed March 12, 2011).

172 Hedy Muntz, *History*.

173 State of Ohio Department of Health, "Certificate of Death," Columbus, OH: 1942.

174 Wikipedia, the Free Encyclopedia, "Dementia Praecox," http:// en.wikipedia.org/wiki/Dementia_praecox (accessed September 12, 2011).

175 Census, Thirteenth Census, 1910, s.v. "Walter Frank Muntz" (accessed June 28, 2011).

176 Harrison Circuit Court, "On Petition."

177 Hedy Muntz, Unpublished Letter to Laura Muntz Derr, in author's collection, undated.

178 Hedy Wright Shaw Muntz and Charles Edward Muntz Sr., interviewed by author (Cynthiana, Kentucky: February 25–26, 1997), transcript and CD recording owned by Laura M. Derr, 5.

179 Charles Edward Muntz Jr. (grandson of Ray Edward Muntz),E-Mail Conversation with author, September 13, 2011.

180 Laura M. Derr, Unpublished Journal Entry, Journal of Laura M. Derr, September 18, 1972.

181 Naff, "A Comprehensive Index of Marriage Records (1894–1947)," www.HarrisonCountyKY.US.

182 Mary Alice Bolen (daughter of James Kenneth Muntz),Telephone Conversation with author, March 5, 2011.

183 Social Security Death Index, "James K. Muntz," 315-16-6793 (Indiana, before 1951), Ancestry.com. http://www.ancestry.com (accessed June 12, 2010).

184 Robert Muntz, E-Mail conversation with author, February 5, 2011.

185 Harrison County Court, "In the Matter of Granting Administration of Geo. N. Muntz Deceased."

186 Commonwealth of Kentucky State Board of Health Bureau of Vital Statistics, "Certificate of Death."

187 "Died at Home Sunday Night," *Shelbyville Republican* (Shelbyville, IN: Shelby County Public Library), December 19, 1927.

188 Census, Fifteenth Census, 1930, Cincinnati, Hamilton, Ohio, s.v. "Clara Whitaker" (accessed March 7, 2011).

189 Rites Held for Mrs. Zikes," *Shelbyville News* (Shelbyville, IN: Shelby County Public Library), January 13, 1975.

190 "Mrs. Vol Whitaker Dies at Home," *Shelby Democrat* (Shelbyville, IN: Shelby County Public Library), September 15, 1938.

191 Judy Gabbard (daughter of Clara Muntz Whitaker), Telephone Conversation with author, July 16, 2011.

192 "Herbert E. Zike," *Shelbyville News*, August 15, 1986.

193 Hedy Muntz, Unpublished Letter.

Reflections

194 Hedy and Charles Edward Muntz Interview, February 25–26, 1997, 7.

195 Ibid., 12.

196 Ibid., 14.

197 Ibid., 8–9.

198 Laura M. Derr, Unpublished Journal Entry, Journal of Laura M. Derr, November 26, 1984.

Bibliography

Axton, W.F. *Tobacco and Kentucky*. Lexington, Kentucky: The University Press of Kentucky, 1975.

Breen, T.H. *Tobacco Culture: The Mentality of the Great Tidewater Planters on the Eve of Revolution*. Princeton, 1987.

Campbell, Tracy. *The Politics of Despair*. Lexington, Kentucky: The University Press of Kentucky, 1993.

Commonwealth of Kentucky State Board of Health Bureau of Vital Statistics. "Viola Muntz Certificate of Death." Frankfort, Kentucky, 1911. #9199.

Commonwealth of Kentucky. Harrison County School District Records. Census Report of District No. 3, State of Kentucky, County of Harrison. For School Year Ending June 30 1896 and 1897. Cynthiana, Kentucky.

Davis, R.B. "Tobacco Culture," *Eastern Reflector*. February 19, 1890. Greenville, NC: East Carolina University. http://150.216.68.252:8080/adore-djatoka/djatoka/viewer.html?pid=ncgre000/00000019/00018975/00018975_ac_0001.jp2&end=4 (accessed 2004).

Derr, Laura M. "E-Mail Conversation with Barbara Ritchie Paiva." May 11, 2010.

Derr, Laura M. "E-Mail Conversation with Charles Edward Muntz Jr." September 13, 2011.

Derr, Laura M. "E-Mail Conversation with Karen Lee Ritchie Schimak." April 22, 2010.

Derr, Laura M. "E-Mail conversation with Robert Muntz." February 5, 2011.

Derr, Laura M. "Interview with Jane Muntz Kearns." Cynthiana, Kentucky: June 17, 2011.

Derr, Laura M. "Oral History Interview with Hedy Wright Shaw Muntz and Charles Edward Muntz Sr. Cynthiana, Kentucky: February 25–26, 1997. Transcript and CD recording owned by Laura M. Derr.

Derr, Laura M. "Telephone Conversation with Barbara Ritchie Paiva." December 2011.

Derr, Laura M. "Telephone Conversation with Judy Gabbard." July 16, 2011.

Derr, Laura M. "Telephone Conversation with Mary Alice Bolen." March 5, 2011.

Derr, Laura M. "Unpublished Journal Entry." Journal of Laura M. Derr. 1972 and 1984.

Duvall, Jeffrey. "Knowing about the Tobacco: Women, Burley, and Farming in the Central Ohio River Valley." *The Register of the Kentucky Historical Society 108*, no. 4 (Autumn 2010): 317-346.

Encyclopaedia Britannica, 1911. www.1911encyclopediabritannica.org/Tobacco (accessed October 21, 2006).

Harrison County Circuit Court. Kentucky Department of Libraries and Archives. Frankfort, Kentucky. Box 57.

Harrison County Court Examining Trial. Kentucky Department of Libraries and Archives. Frankfort, Kentucky. Box 65.

Harrison County Court. Harrison County Deeds and County Clerk Records. Cynthiana, Kentucky, 1894-1910.

Kleber, John E. ed. *The Kentucky Encyclopedia.* Third Printing. Lexington, Kentucky: University Press of Kentucky, 1992.

Muntz Jr., Charles E. "Interview with Eloise Judy (wife of Edgar Judy, son of Virgil and Laura Belle Judy." Millersburg, Kentucky, October 20, 2009.

Muntz, Hedy S. *History of the Muntz Family.*Unpublished manuscript. Cynthiana, Kentucky, 1988.

Muntz, Hedy S. "Unpublished Letter to Laura Muntz Derr." Author's collection. undated.

Naff, Philip A. "M.C. Swinford." *Biographies of Harrison County, Kentucky.* http://home.comcast.net/~harrisoncountykyus/people/biographies-s-t-u-surnames.htm (accessed February 9, 2012).

Naff, Philip A. "A Comprehensive Index of Marriage Records (1894–1947)." http://home.comcast.net/~harrisoncountykyus/records/marriage-records.htm (accessed 2007).

Perrin, William Henry, ed. *History of Bourbon, Scott, Harrison and Nicholas Counties of Kentucky.* Chicago: O.L. Baskin & Co., 1882.

Searles, David P. *A College for Appalachia: Alice Lloyd on Caney Creek*. Lexington, Kentucky: The University Press of Kentucky, 1995.

Shelby Democrat. Shelbyville, Indiana: Shelby County Public Library. 1938.

Shelbyville News. Shelbyville, Indiana: Shelby County Public Library. 1975 and 1986.

Shelbyville Republican. Shelbyville, Indiana: Shelby County Public Library, 1927.

Social Security Death Index. "James K. Muntz." 315-16-6793. Indiana, before 1951. Ancestry.com. http://search.ancestry.com/cgi-bin/sse.dll?db=ssdi&rank=1&new=1&so=3&MSAV=0&msT=1&gss=ms_db&gsfn=James+Kenneth&gsln=Muntz&gskw=315-16-6793+&dbOnly=_F00032DD%7C_F00032DD_x&uidh=pj5 (accessed June 12, 2010).

State of Ohio Department of Health. "Rosa F. Cheney Certificate of Death." Columbus, Ohio, 1942.

Swinford, Mac. *Kentucky Lawyer*. Lexington, Kentucky: The University Press of Kentucky, 2008.

The Cynthiana Democrat. Cynthiana, Kentucky: Cynthiana Public Library. Microfilm1909,1910, and 1928.

The Log Cabin. Cynthiana, Kentucky: Cynthiana Public Library. Microfilm 1906–1911.

U.S. Census Bureau, *Ninth Census, 1870*. Ancestry.com. http://www.ancestry.com (accessed April 22, 2011).

U.S. Census Bureau, *Tenth Census, 1880*. Ancestry. com. http://www.ancestry.com (accessed 2006).

U.S Census Bureau, *Twelfth Census, 1900*. Ancestry. com. http://www.ancestry.com (accessed 2011).

U.S Census Bureau, *Thirteenth Census, 1910*. Ancestry.com. http://www.ancestry.com (accessed 2006).

U.S. Census Bureau, *Fourteenth Census, 1920*. Ancestry.com. http://www.ancestry.com (accessed June 10, 2010).

U.S. Census Bureau, *Fifteenth Census, 1930*. Ancestry.com. http://www.ancestry.com (accessed March 12, 2011).

van Willigan, John and Susan C. Eastwood. *Tobacco Culture: Farming Kentucky's Burley Belt*. Lexington, Kentucky: The University Press of Kentucky, 1998.

Wikipedia, the Free Encyclopedia. "Dementia Praecox." http://en.wikipedia.org/wiki/Dementia_praecox (accessed September 12, 2011).

19813335R00105

Made in the USA
Charleston, SC
13 June 2013